Grome Terrain Modeling with Ogre3D, UDK, and Unity3D

Create massive terrains and export them to the most popular game engines

Richard A. Hawley

PUBLISHING

BIRMINGHAM - MUMBAI

Grome Terrain Modeling with Ogre3D, UDK, and Unity3D

First published: February 2013

Production Reference: 1110213

Published by Packt Publishing Ltd.
Livery Place
35 Livery Street
Birmingham B3 2PB, UK.

ISBN 978-1-84969-939-6

www.packtpub.com

Cover Image by Neha Rajappan (neha.rajappan1@gmail.com)

Credits

Author
Richard A. Hawley

Reviewer
Adrian Licuriceanu

Stefano Provenzano

Acquisition Editor
Mary Nadar

Content Commissioning Editor
Meeta Rajani

Technical Editor
Worrell Lewis

Project Coordinator
Esha Thakker

Proofreader
Mario Cecere

Indexer
Monica Ajmera

Graphics
Valentina D'silva

Production Coordinator
Pooja Chiplunkar

Cover Work
Pooja Chiplunkar

About the Author

Richard Hawley started programming in the early 1980s at the start of the home computer craze with the Sinclair ZX-81. Before leaving high school he had worked on three game projects for Assassin Software and later worked on conversions of classic strategy board games for 8- to 16-bit machines. He went on to develop end-user tools for popular flight simulations including Empire Interactive's Enemy Engaged helicopter series and the highly successful Origin Jane's Longbow series (MissioneerPlus).

He's the director of Tricubic Studios, a small UK company dedicated to creating simulation and training environments using off-the-shelf 3D engines including Unity and Leadwerks. Together with technical artist David Hopkinson (Total War: English Civil War conversion) and physics guru Fred Naar (creator of Helicopter Total Realism for Microsoft Flight Simulator X) they are collectively known for their work on helicopter simulations.

I would like to thank my wife Dorothy for putting up with my long sabbaticals in front of the computer and my kids who have grown used to becoming experimental subjects on family board gaming nights.

People I've had the privilege to work with; David Hopkinson for being a patient sounding board throughout our joint creative endeavors, his talent of being able to make silk purses out of sow's ears is a testament to his ingenuity. I'd also like to thank Fred Naar who not only created the most amazing and unique helicopter physics engine but who also is a really nice guy. Other thanks go to Rob Hardaway for years of designing impossible mission scenarios, but mostly for hanging around at flight simulation shows being mistaken for me (which I'm more than happy about since he's six foot tall and fighter-pilot handsome).

Thanks to Adrian Licuriceanu at Quad Software for his technical support with Grome, and for playing the role of accuracy police for this book.

Finally, a big thank you to the simulation community, SimHQ, and various individuals that continue to be supportive in the face of my endless and annoying prevarication and distractions (of which this book is but one of them). Sorry!

Art is never finished, only abandoned.

About the Reviewers

Adrian Licuriceanu started programming from an early age. Later, in both high school and college, he studied computer science and from the very beginning was fascinated with graphics programming. After graduating from college, in 2000, when a funding opportunity arrived, he founded Quad Software with the aim of creating technology for Massively Multiplayer Games. During the 5 years that he was the lead programmer he developed two engines used for MMO games. Later, he built on the previous experience to create Grome, a game-level editor currently employed by many professional studios. After two years of internal development, together with a small team of programmers, they managed to bring Grome to commercial quality and successfully launched the product in 2007. Currently, Grome is at its third version and it is used by many top professional game studios, simulation industry corporations, and universities. After another two years from the initial Grome launch, Adrian and his team made public the Graphite engine, the rendering middleware companion to Grome, an engine that can be used to render the complex scenes Grome can produce.

Stefano Provenzano is an Italian senior consultant and software engineer, who has worked on several projects in different fields of computer science including 3D real-time engines for PC and Playstation videogames, visual simulation and virtual prototyping, web application, and system integration.

In 2006, Stefano started his own software development and consulting company, Shin Software. Currently, Stefano is working on RIA and hi-quality mobile/web 3D real-time applications using Unity3D.

> To my wife Irene and our children Davide and Pietro, your love gives me the strength to work and study hard.

www.PacktPub.com

Support files, eBooks, discount offers and more

You might want to visit www.PacktPub.com for support files and downloads related to your book.

Did you know that Packt offers eBook versions of every book published, with PDF and ePub files available? You can upgrade to the eBook version at www.PacktPub.com and as a print book customer, you are entitled to a discount on the eBook copy. Get in touch with us at service@packtpub.com for more details.

At www.PacktPub.com, you can also read a collection of free technical articles, sign up for a range of free newsletters and receive exclusive discounts and offers on Packt books and eBooks.

http://PacktLib.PacktPub.com

Do you need instant solutions to your IT questions? PacktLib is Packt's online digital book library. Here, you can access, read and search across Packt's entire library of books.

Why Subscribe?

- Fully searchable across every book published by Packt
- Copy and paste, print and bookmark content
- On demand and accessible via web browser

Free Access for Packt account holders

If you have an account with Packt at www.PacktPub.com, you can use this to access PacktLib today and view nine entirely free books. Simply use your login credentials for immediate access.

Table of Contents

Preface

Role-playing games and simulations can feature vast landscapes. Whether shaped by imagination or real geography the amount of data is potentially huge. GROME is ideally
suited for ground modeling of large terrains with memory paging and procedural-generation techniques.

Now in its third generation, GROME 3.1 has evolved to meet the specific needs of developers and artists creating detailed, dynamically-loaded landscapes. New features support the creation of simple meshes from highly-detailed terrain suitable for use in mobile games and improved flowmap generation.

Used in the production of console games and simulation labs worldwide, GROME 3.1 is supplied with Software Development Kits (SDKs) to aid the production process. Like any specialist tool, it can be somewhat intimidating to the newcomer. This book is designed
to assist readers, new to using GROME 3.1, and guide them through in a logical order.

What this book covers

Chapter 1, *Creating Virtual Landscapes*, looks at the concept of map storage in games, limitations imposed by 3D technology, and starting a new GROME project.

Chapter 2, *GROME Workspace*, walks us through the major parts of the user interface that we will be using through the rest of the book. Then we begin the process of creating "zones" which are the basic components of a terrain.

Chapter 3, *Heightmaps*, looks at the bulk of the tools used for modeling heightmaps; using brush and automatic procedural techniques combined. We round this off with a look at using masks to protect regions from modification. This also contains the obligatory "Hello World" example, but in heightmap form.

Chapter 4, Textures and Lighting, covers using textures and masks combined to blend different layers together. We also look at flowmaps, automatic mask generation, filters, shadow maps, and light maps. Additionally, we look at color baking for squashing multiple texture layers into one, for mobile support and normal maps.

Chapter 5, Bring Me a Shrubbery, explores the special support for vegetation using billboards and instances of 3D objects. Ground details greatly enhance a scene, as hardware becomes more powerful, more details can be added. Ground cover can be generated procedurally to create huge areas of ground detail.

Chapter 6, Water, River, and Roads, walks us through the water toolset, creating multiple water layers, material properties, adding shorelines, and creating roads using the spline tools.

Chapter 7, Exporting to Unity, UDK, and Ogre 3D, helps us export basic terrains using several techniques for Unity3D. Then we cover a 3D mesh export for UDK as a basic ground layer. Then finally we use the Graphite exporter which creates near 100 percent compatible GROME scenes when using the GromeOgre source code.

What you need for this book

A licensed installation of GROME 3.x or an evaluation (which has no export or saving facility but can be used for most of the presented tutorials). For download details, please see the official vendor's website:

www.quadsoftware.com

Unity3D game engine is available free for non-commercial use from:

www.unity3d.com

Unreal Development Kit (UDK) is available for non-commercial use from:

www.udk.com

Ogre3D is a free open source rendering engine. Visual Studio 2005 to 2010 can be used to compile any of the GROME examples in addition to the Graphite library which is available to licensed GROME clients. Ogre3D can be downloaded from:

www.ogre3d.org

Please be sure to read the licensing terms when downloading and installing these engines. Your computer should also meet the following specifications:

- Windows XP SP2 or higher
- 4 MB of RAM, or more, if using a 64-bit OS (recommended)
- Graphics card with 256 MB VRAM and at least four texture units

Who this book is for

If you're a developer or technical artist looking for a companion guide to walk you through GROME 3.1 then this book will help you through those early steps through practical use.

Due to the sheer scope of GROME 3.1, it's not possible to produce a definitive guide to everything in the space of a book this size. However, GROME is supplied with documentation covering these more technical aspects such as the plugin SDKs and scripting. It's hoped that this book goes some way to getting you to the level where the user is comfortable enough to explore these features.

As mainstream game engines like Unity3D add more features supporting mobile platforms, independent developers are expanding the scope of what kind of games they can produce. GROME's ability to take huge datasets designed for larger platforms and export them as suitable meshes for mobile platforms becomes a welcome tool in the artist's toolbox. This text will show you how.

Conventions

In this book, you will find a number of styles of text that distinguish between different kinds of information. Here are some examples of these styles, and an explanation of their meaning.

New terms and **important words** are shown in bold. Words that you see on the screen, in menus or dialog boxes for example, appear in the text like this: "click on the **Apply to All** button to assign these settings to the current viewports".

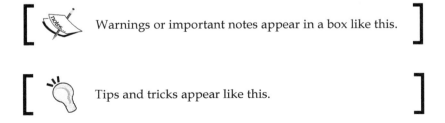

Warnings or important notes appear in a box like this.

Tips and tricks appear like this.

Reader feedback

Feedback from our readers is always welcome. Let us know what you think about this book—what you liked or may have disliked. Reader feedback is important for us to develop titles that you really get the most out of.

To send us general feedback, simply send an e-mail to feedback@packtpub.com, and mention the book title via the subject of your message.

If there is a topic that you have expertise in and you are interested in either writing or contributing to a book, see our author guide on www.packtpub.com/authors.

Customer support

Now that you are the proud owner of a Packt book, we have a number of things to help you to get the most from your purchase.

Downloading the example code

You can download the example code files for all Packt books you have purchased from your account at http://www.packtpub.com. If you purchased this book elsewhere, you can visit http://www.packtpub.com/support and register to have the files e-mailed directly to you.

Errata

Although we have taken every care to ensure the accuracy of our content, mistakes do happen. If you find a mistake in one of our books—maybe a mistake in the text or the code—we would be grateful if you would report this to us. By doing so, you can save other readers from frustration and help us improve subsequent versions of this book. If you find any errata, please report them by visiting http://www.packtpub.com/submit-errata, selecting your book, clicking on the **errata submission form** link, and entering the details of your errata. Once your errata are verified, your submission will be accepted and the errata will be uploaded on our website, or added to any list of existing errata, under the Errata section of that title. Any existing errata can be viewed by selecting your title from http://www.packtpub.com/support.

Piracy

Piracy of copyright material on the Internet is an ongoing problem across all media. At Packt, we take the protection of our copyright and licenses very seriously. If you come across any illegal copies of our works, in any form, on the Internet, please provide us with the location address or website name immediately so that we can pursue a remedy.

Please contact us at copyright@packtpub.com with a link to the suspected pirated material.

We appreciate your help in protecting our authors, and our ability to bring you valuable content.

Questions

You can contact us at questions@packtpub.com if you are having a problem with any aspect of the book, and we will do our best to address it.

Creating Virtual Landscapes

1

Tools are everything in game development today. Let me quickly tell you a story. Back in 1983 home computers were simple enough that you could create a virtual city (made of blocks) using nothing much more than pen and paper to scratch out lines of hexadecimal code. The code would then be entered (by hand) over several coffee fuelled evenings and assuming you got every number correct and didn't suffer a tape loading error you could make amazing new worlds. If this sounds primitive and a lot of hard work, well it was. The technological equivalent of scratching out lines of dirt with a plough. Pioneering stuff.

Modern three-dimensional games are several orders of magnitude more complex than Sandy White's 1983 Ant Attack on the Sinclair ZX Spectrum. To create lush visuals expected from current games, we rely on a host of tools to generate content at different stages of production. Quite often, terrain is the canvas on which content is painted, if you think about it, while you might play a game and think how great the scenery looks, you're not necessarily looking at the terrain but rather the textures, vegetation, buildings and everything else that artist has constructed around it. Before we dive into using GROME we're going to cover some common caveats that apply to most game engines. In this chapter we're going to look at:

- Describing a world in data
- Texture sizes
- Game world scales
- Starting a new GROME project

Describing a world in data

Just like modern games, early games like Ant Attack required data that described in some meaningful way how the landscape was to appear. The eerie city landscape of "Antchester" (shown in the following screenshot) was constructed in memory as a 128 x 128 byte grid, the first 128 bytes defined the upper-left wall, and the 128 byte row below that, and so on. Each of these bytes described the vertical arrangement of blocks in lower six bits, for game logic purposes the upper two bits were used for game sprites.

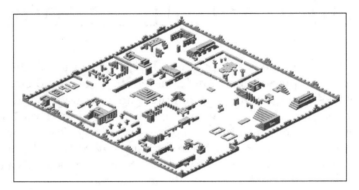

Heightmaps are common ground

The arrangement of numbers in a grid pattern is still extensively used to represent terrain. We call these grids "maps" and they are popular by virtue of being simple to use and manipulate. A long way from "Antchester", maps can now be measured in megabytes or Gigabytes (around 20GB is needed for the whole earth at 30 meter resolution). Each value in the map represents the height of the terrain at that location.

These kinds of maps are known as heightmaps. However, any information that can be represented in the grid pattern can use maps. Additional maps can be used by 3D engines to tell it how to mix many textures together; this is a common terrain painting technique known as "splatting". Splats describe the *amount* of blending between texture layers. Another kind of map might be used for lighting, adding light, or shadows to an area of the map. We also find in some engines something called visibility maps which hide parts of the terrain; for example we might want to add holes or caves into a landscape. Coverage maps might be used to represent objects such as grasses, different vegetation layers might have some kind of map the engine uses to draw 3D objects onto the terrain surface. GROME allows us to create and edit all of these kinds of maps and export them, with a little bit of manipulation we can port this information into most game engines. Whatever the technique used by an engine to paint the terrain, height-maps are fairly universal in how they are used to describe topography.

The following is an example of a heightmap loaded into an image viewer. It appears as a gray scale image, the intensity of each pixel represents a height value at that location on the map.

This map represents a 100 square kilometer area of north-west Afghanistan used in a flight simulation.

GROME like many other terrain editing tools uses heightmaps to transport terrain information. Typically importing the heightmap as a gray scale image using common file formats such as TIFF, PNG, or BMP. When it's time to export the terrain project you have similar options to save.

This commonality is the basis of using GROME as a tool for many different engines. There's nothing to stop you from making changes to an exported heightmap using image editing software. The GROME plugin system and SDK permit you to make your own custom exporter for any unsupported formats. So long as we can deal with the material and texture format requirements for our host 3D engine we can integrate GROME into the art pipeline. Well, easier said than done, quite often this is the tricky part which we'll get to at the end of this book.

Texture sizes

Using textures for heightmap information does have limitations. The largest "safe" size for a texture is considered 4096 x 4096 although some of the older 3D cards would have problems with anything higher than 2048 x 2048. Also, host 3D engines often require texture dimensions to be a power of 2. A table of recommended dimensions for images follow:

SafeTexture dimensions
64 x 64
128 x 128
256 x 256
512 x 512
1024 x 1024
2048 x 2048
4096 x 4096

512 x 512 provides efficient trade-off between resolution and performance and is the default value for GROME operations.

If you're familiar with this already then great, you might see questions posted on forums about texture corruption or materials not looking correct. Sometimes these problems are the result of not conforming to this arrangement. Also, you'll see these numbers crop up a few times in GROME's drop-down property boxes. To avoid any potential problems it is wise to ensure any textures you use in your projects conform to these specifications. One exception is **Unreal Development Kit (UDK)** in which you'll see numbers such as 257 x 257 used, we'll discuss this in *Chapter 7, Exporting to Unity, UDK, and Ogre 3D*.

If you have a huge amount of terrain data that you need to import for a project you can use the texture formats mentioned earlier but I recommend using RAW formats if possible. If your project is based on real-world topography then importing DTED or GeoTIFF data will extract geographical information such as latitude, longitude, and number of arc seconds represented by the terrain.

> **Digital Terrain Elevation Data (DTED)**
>
> A file format used by geographers and mappers to map the height of a terrain. Often used to import real-world topography into flight simulations. **Shuttle Radar Topography Mission (SRTM)** data is easily obtained and converted.

The huge world problem

Huge landscapes may require a lot of memory, potentially more than a 3D card can handle. In game consoles memory is a scarce resource, on mobile devices transferring the app and storing is a factor. Even on a cutting edge PC large datasets will eat into that onboard memory especially when we get down to designing and building them using high-resolution data. Requesting actions that eat up your system memory may cause the application to fail. We can use GROME to create vast worlds without worrying too much about memory. This is done by taking advantage of how GROME manages data through a process of splitting terrain into "zones" and swapping it out to disk. This swapping is similar to how operating systems move memory to disk and reload it on demand. By default whenever you import large DTED files GROME will break the region into multiple zones and hide them. Someone new to GROME might be confused by a lengthy file import operation only to be presented with a seemingly empty project space.

When creating terrain for engines such as Unity, UDK, Ogre3D, and others you should keep in mind their own technical limitations of what they can reasonably import.

Most of these engines are built for small scale scenes. While GROME doesn't impose any specific unit of measure on your designs, one unit equals one meter is a good rule of thumb. Many third-party models are made to this scale. However it's up to the artist to pick a unit of scale and importantly, be consistent.

Keep in mind many 3D engines are limited by two factors:

* Floating point math precision
* Z-buffer (depth buffer) precision

Floating point precision

As a general rule anything larger than 20,000 units away from the world origin in any direction is going to exhibit precision errors. This manifests as vertex jitter whenever vertices are rotated and transformed by large values. The effects are not something you can easily work around. Changing the scale of the object shifts the error to another decimal point. Normally in engines that specialize in rendering large worlds they either use a camera-relative rendering or some kind of paging system. Unity and UDK are not inherently capable of camera-relative rendering but a method of paging is possible to employ. There are techniques available such as a treadmill style terrain system but these are beyond the scope of this book to demonstrate.

Depth buffer precision

The other issue associated with large scene rendering is z-fighting. The depth buffer is a normally invisible part of a scene used to determine what part is hidden by another, depth-testing. Whenever a pixel is written to a scene buffer the z component is saved in the depth buffer. Typically this buffer has 16 bits of precision, meaning you have a linear depth of 0 to 65,536. This depth value is based on the 3D camera's view range (the difference between the camera near and far distance). Z-fighting occurs when objects appear to be co-planer polygons written into the z-buffer with similar depth values causing them to "fight" for visibility. This flickering is an indicator that the scene and camera settings need to be rethought. Often the easy fix is to increase the z-buffer precision by increasing the camera's near distance. The downside is that this can clip very near objects.

GROME will let you create such large worlds. Its own Graphite engine handles them well. Most 3D engines are designed for smaller first and third-person games which will have a practical limit of around 10 to 25 square kilometers (1 meter = 1 unit). GROME can mix levels of detail quite easily, different regions of the terrain have their own mesh density. If for example you have a map on an island, you will want lots of detail for the land and less in the sea region. However, game engines such as Unity, UDK, and Ogre3 Dare are not easily adapted to deal with such variability in the terrain mesh since they are optimized to render a large triangular grid of uniform size. Instead, we use techniques to fake extra detail and bake it into our terrain textures, dramatically reducing the triangle count in the process. Using a combination of Normal Maps and Mesh Layers in GROME we can create the illusion of more detail than there is at a distance.

Normal map

A Normal is a unit vector (a vector with a total length of one) perpendicular to a surface. When a texture is used as a Normal map, the red, green, and blue channels represent the vector (x,y,z). These are used to generate the illusion of more detail by creating a bumpy looking surface. Also known as bump-maps. Normal map generation is covered in *Chapter 4, Textures and Lighting*.

Planning our first project – the brief

For purposes of demonstration we're going to be working on a hypothetical game as part of a team. We have a design document and the art lead has tasked us with creating the exterior map for the "Volcano Lair" of the evil Doctor Yes and his sidekick, Professor Maybe. Our game features the propitious handsome hero "Guy Goodwin" on a mission to thwart the evil plans of an organization called "DEAD Certainty". The team lead is really enthused and promises it will be great, not really.

Our task is to turn concept and sketches into a detailed virtual environment using GROME as part of the toolset so we can export it for different game engines.

Already we can take away some information about what we can build. The characters sound over the top, the tone of this game is clearly humored, larger than life. It's a first-person game meaning ground detail will need to be pretty high in player accessible areas. This part of the game takes place on an island which has the following key locations as listed in our brief:

- A volcano (with interior access via a bunker)
- Professor Maybe's villa or laboratory
- A power station
- Coastal docks
- River with a boat event
- Airfield (with getaway plane)

Creating a rough sketch of our map, we get a feel for relative positions and scale of the terrain we need. We keep main story locations clustered around the origin of the world to reduce precision problems on the destination platforms.

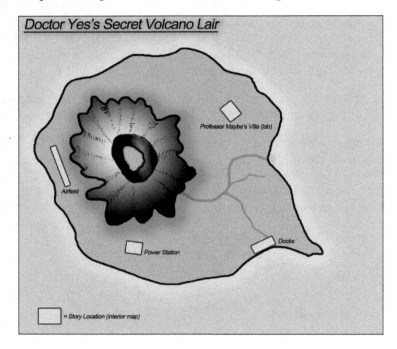

What we can take away from such a sketch is the rough outline of major features, in this case the shape of the island. We can import this at a later stage and use it as a mask in GROME when creating the heightmap.

Generating terrain can be done procedurally which is what we're going to do for our game example. Then we'll use our sketch to create masks we can import into GROME. These work just like masks in programs like Photoshop and GIMP.

If we need to go back and change the position of key locations (for example; the project lead might want to move two places closer together to speed up story progression), we can do this quite easily in GROME using masks or a clone brush tool which we will explore later.

Starting GROME

Depending on your host operating system you should launch either the 32-bit or 64-bit Version. If you have more than 4 GB of memory installed and a 64-bit edition of the Windows operating system then you should take advantage of running GROME (64 bit), every bit of extra memory helps (no pun intended). If you need to work with very detailed scenes you should opt for this work environment as it will pay off in terms of swap times. These examples are created using the 32-bit edition which look identical. Let's get started.

1. Launch GROME 3.1, when greeted with the quick start dialog click on the **Create a new project** button.

2. You'll see a **New Scene** dialog like the following screenshot. Since we want to get started creating our volcano lair we'll call our project volcano_lair. You'll notice a number of icons grouped under **Project Type**, the type determines what kind of features you can add to the project. For now we'll just select **Complete Scene** which is everything.

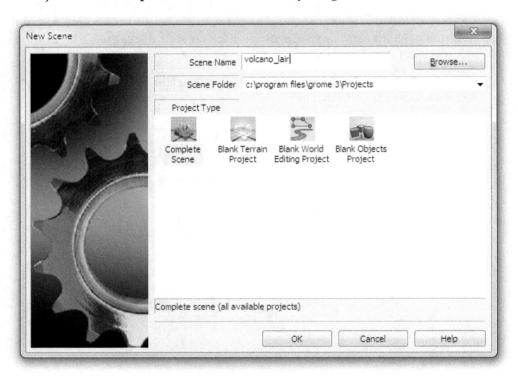

After a short moment you'll be presented with an, initially, intimidating interface and an empty scene.

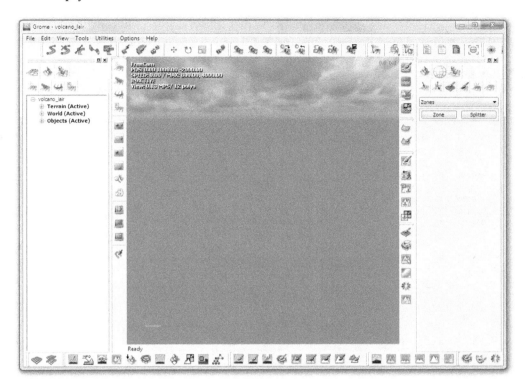

Before you start to panic, the imposing interface buttons bordering the work area are common editor functions we'll be accessing from other parts of the interface. By default the GROME interface is arranged with the tablet user in mind. If your default view is split into four viewports you can change it to a single viewport through the **OPTIONS** menu. Select **Preferences** and set the viewports in the dialog as given in the following screenshot. Be sure to click on the **Apply to All** button to assign these settings to the current viewports.

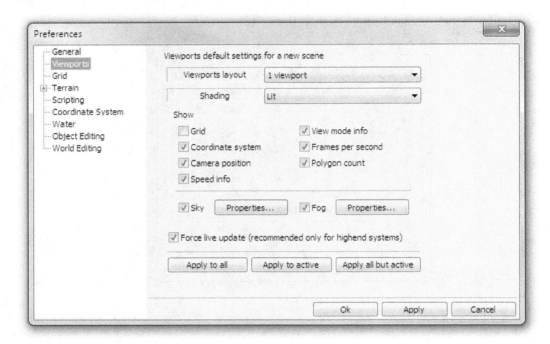

Summary

In this chapter we looked at heightmaps and how they allow us to import and export to other programs and engines. We touched upon world sizes and limitations commonly found in 3D engines. We then examined a brief for a hypothetical game, sketched out a map in preparation before finally creating a new GROME project file. In the next chapter, we'll look at how the interface is arranged and work through the toolset as we get to grips with the interface.

In the next chapter, we're going to look at the workspace and the all-important layer stack.

2
GROME Workspace

With pencils sharpened and a steaming pot of fresh coffee we're now ready to jump into the GROME interface. The user interface might appear intimidating with dozens of icons framing the window. We're going to focus on the main parts of the interface shown in the image as follows:

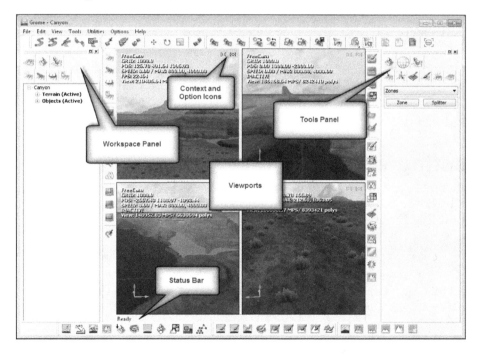

Viewports

The viewports have resizable dividers; you can drag them around individually and toggle between the split and tabbed views by double-clicking on them.

Located in the top-right corner of every viewport are two icons shown in the following screenshot. The left icon brings up the "Context" menu, this shows operations applicable to the currently selected object. The second is the "View" menu that displays options for adjusting the camera and rendering modes (textured, wireframe, lit, fog, top, left, perspective, walk, and so on).

When the viewport is active, standard WSAD keys move the camera. Holding down *Shift* increases the movement speed. To move the camera up and down use the *E* and *C* keys respectively. There are many useful keyboard shortcuts for navigating scenes. You can view these by going to **Menu Options | Customize Keyboard**; choose **Group | Application** and change the drop-down box that reads **Category** to **Viewport**. This will display a list of all keyboard shortcuts for the camera.

Depending on the scale of our scene camera movement might be either too fast or too slow. To quickly adjust the standard movement speed of the camera you can; press *Ctrl* and move the mouse wheel up to increase the camera speed, conversely press *CTRL* and move the mouse wheel down to decrease the camera speed.

Selecting objects

Edit functions need an active selection. You can select whatever is under the mouse pointer by holding down *Ctrl* and the left mouse click. This is an additive selection; select multiple zones by repeatedly clicking while holding down *Ctrl*.

You can select everything in a rectangular region by holding down *Ctrl* and the left mouse button down.

To select all objects press *Ctrl + A*. To deselect everything press *Ctrl + D*. There are many other selection methods which are covered in the GROME documentation that I encourage the reader to explore.

Workspace panel

All of the editing functions we'll be using are located in two main areas of the interface; the Tool panel and the Workspace panel. Both of these panels are headed by two rows of tabs which we make good use of, so get familiar with them.

The first row is like a master mode and the second row of tabs gives access to the submode. The Workspace panel is located to the left-hand side of the viewports in the default interface layout.

Workspace tab

Workspace is an overview of what our current scene contains, scene settings, layers, and any objects we're using.

Scene tab

The scene tab allows access to how a scene is rendered and contains settings for the camera field of view (FOV), camera range, lighting, and fog. This is illustrated in the following image:

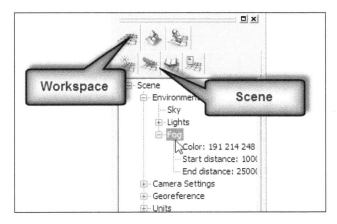

We can adjust how a fog is rendered by changing the color and range through the scene.

1. Click on the Workspace master mode (first tab icon).
2. Select the **Scene** tab to bring up the scene tree.
3. Right-click on the **Fog** node and select **Properties** from the pop-up menu.

You can add a little blue to the fog color to make the scene a little more realistic and depending on how big our scene is, we might need to change the fog distances.

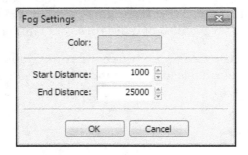

You can adjust the camera FOV (field of view) and the first-person camera mode walk-height. The walk-height is specified in world units. If you're working in meters you might want to set this value to 2. By default this is set to 180 which is perfect if you're working in centimeters (1.8 meters is about human height).

The other nodes are not going to see much use. **Georeference** is an advanced option used to embed information about real-world positions in your scenery. The unit's node will only affect how data is exported to some formats; it won't scale your scene in any way.

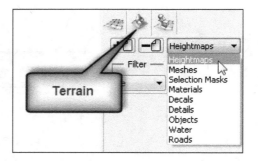

Layer stack

The predominant tab on the Workspace panel is the **Terrain** layer stack pane. Layers in GROME work in a similar fashion to other image editing software. Layer content is applied in a bottom-up fashion. An example layer stack would ideally have an imported heightmap in the bottom-most layer; on top of which we add special features such as hills followed by a noise layer. If instead of adding landscaping features such as rivers and roads (which may need to be adjusted later), we add layers for each of them, it would give us the freedom to edit without modifying the base terrain.

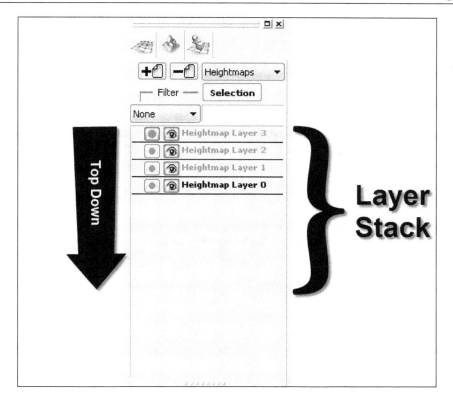

The two folded-page icons are used for adding and deleting layers. Clicking on the "+", add layer, button creates an empty layer on top of the stack. Each layer is displayed with two icons and its default name (for example, **Heightmap Layer 0**). The first icon is the "ARM" button; when this is active (red) it indicates that edits can be applied to this layer. The following image shows a layer with the armed and visible icons active.

When the "ARM" button is gray then tools have no effect on this layer, this is often necessary as we usually only want to apply tools to a few of them. The second icon is the layer visibility button. Toggle this to show and hide the effects of this layer.

Layer type selector

The drop-down box next to the layer buttons selects the type of layer to display. The full list of available layer types are given as follows:

- **Heightmaps** represent terrain topography and can be merged together as layers.

- **Meshes** are 3D models generated from the terrain grid, this is useful for iPhone and Android platforms or engines that don't have any native terrain support.

- **Selection Masks** are used to protect areas of your terrain when performing operations.

- **Materials** are the texture and color layers. Creative use of texturing, shaders, and blending of layers can yield impressive results.

- **Decals** are special polygons that are projected flat onto the terrain surface.

- **Details** are high-performance 3D models. For example, many copies of the same tree model are used to make forests. Detail layers are used to place rocks, grass, trees, and so on.

- **Objects** are individual 3D models, buildings, signs, rubble, and so on. You can make good use of object layers for cross-platform requirements.

- **Water layers** are simple planes at a set height. Coverage masks for each zone are exported as a grayscale texture.

- **Roads** are spline-based objects that can modify underlying terrain to fit.

Selection filter

The usefulness of the selection filter will become apparent when you start to build complex scenes requiring careful navigation. If you have hundreds of similar objects in a scene such as a lamppost and you need to find a particular one you can type the name or number into the filter control here.

If you are going to use GROME to place 3D objects into scenes you should think about naming conventions when crafting your scene. Object names can be exported to the host engine, if your game has code that needs to send values to all objects of a certain type then it will help to embed some ID into the object name. You might want to get the team together to plan a suitable object naming scheme if they are to be used in code or game logic. If you have to edit names in the host engine after exporting (such as the Unity3D or UDK editor) all changes will be lost whenever you reexport the project. You might as well fix it at the source early on and get it right.

Tools panel

Located to the right-hand side of the viewport, the tools panel has a lot of features packed into it. Hosting all the content-editing functions, the tools panel is headed by three tabs to select from three kinds of editing. They are given as follows:

- Terrain
- World (Roads)
- Objects (instanced entities)

Most of our work will be done with the Terrain tools. Working from the left-hand side to the right-hand side, the second row of icons are: Create (zone), Modifiers, Selection, Texturing, Details, and Water. This roughly follows the workflow in a GROME project. The Tool panel icons are shown as follows:

Workflow/creation path

Creating landscapes isn't a rigidly defined process. If you had to define a flow through the creation process it would look like the following diagram:

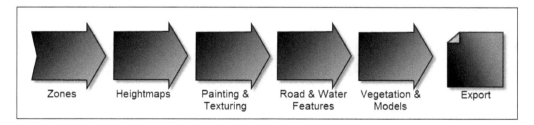

Starting with the creation of zones, we edit our heightmaps, paint and texture the landscape before adding landscape features such as roads, rivers, and vegetation. Finally, we export everything. Depending on our destination platform we might skip one or more of these stages and use native 3D game engine features for them. If the scope of the game is small you might use GROME for heightmap creation and painting everything else in the Unity 3D editor.

It is possible at any time to go back and change the density of a terrain grid if you need more (or less) detail.

Document the export process

Make notes of all the export settings taking screenshots if necessary. You will forget which settings are needed for a particular build. Someone else might need to export the project and will thank you for it. Artists should have a book near them covering technical details of the art content pipeline; this is a good place to keep such information. If you don't have such a book, make one. Coffee ring stains are optional but make it look well used and professional.

Zones

Zones are containers for terrains, objects, masks, and roads, but importantly they define size and terrain resolution. Each one can have its own properties. This allows us to create landscapes with variable amounts of detail according to the needs of a game. You can create zones *anywhere* in the scene; they don't need to be contiguous. Creating very long narrow terrains that follow the length of a river are possible; an "on-rails" game that follows a long winding path does not have a huge regular terrain grid. However, for simple exporting to game engines it is best if we stick to a square arrangement, as game editors don't natively support asymmetric layouts.

The Zone toolbox tab is shown in the following screenshot:

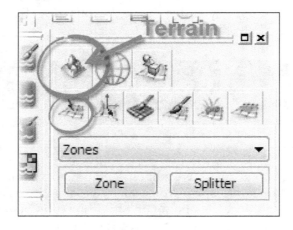

We can create zones in several ways; the easiest is entering size parameters and using the mouse to define an area called the **Active Creation Grid** in the scene.

Click on the **Zone** button to activate the creation process. You'll see the scene divided by a grid (the scale depends on the value of the **Size** parameter when the Zone tool is activated). The parameters in the Terrain Zone panel are important for all the zone creation methods so we'll go over what they mean:

- **Size**: The width and height in world units of the zone when you click on the **Create** button.

- **Tiles no**: The number of tiles (across and down) that will be generated for the zone. A tile is the smallest editable unit in GROME. The number of vertices across the terrain mesh will be this value plus one.

- **Tile size**: This is an alternative way of specifying the resolution of the grid. When you update this value, the number of tiles is automatically updated to be **Size/Tile size**.

To illustrate the relationship between Size, Tile no, and Tile size, refer to following figure which shows three zones created with different parameters.

Most projects will require higher resolution unless you are creating tiles for a flight-simulator where areas of ground detail are mostly flat with satellite images layered on top. Publicly available satellite topography often has a very low resolution, about 30 meters to 200 meters between data points. The following image shows three zones created with different parameters:

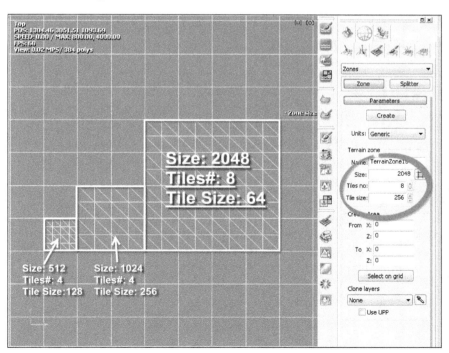

Know the dimensions

If you know the dimensions of the region you need to create, you can enter the corner coordinates in the **Create Area** panel (1 world unit = 1 meter). A 5 km area centered on the world origin can be created with the following values:

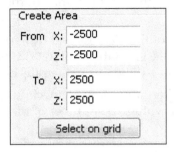

After you have entered the coordinates, clicking on the **Select on grid** button will mark the area in the viewport. To complete the action click on **Create**. GROME will generate the appropriate number of zones to cover the area you specified (width divided by size). If the total width is 5,000 units and the size is set to 500 then 100 zones will be created (10 rows and 10 columns). Each zone will contain the number of tiles specified so ensure the Tile no. is set to something reasonable or you might have memory problems.

Creating zones this way is ideal for game engines as you typically know how big the area you need is in advance.

Zone splitter

This handy function allows us to split selected zones into a specified number of smaller ones. **Split factor** is the number of rows and columns the zone will be split into. The number of splits must match the number of tiles in the zone.

Example – volcano island

As we have a blank project ready to roll, the first thing we need for it (or any new project) is some terrain to play with. Terrain grids are constructed from zones and we are going to start with the first button on the toolbar **Create**. To create terrain for our game we must start with zones.

Our volcano project will need a high level of detail, we're going to make an island of approximately 10 square kilometers. Since we want it to be reasonably detailed, we'll create it with the following values for a 5 square kilometer zone:

Size=5120, Tile no.=512, Tile size=10

Note that our map is not exactly 5 km since we like to use nice computing numbers which are a power of 2. The map measures exactly 5.12 km.

Next we'll mark out a quad of four zones (2 x 2) which will be the base of our map. When we're done with the values and the region we've marked, click on the **Create** button. A layer is automatically created and armed in the Workspace panel on the right-hand side.

We can check zones with *Ctrl + A* (select all). If we want to edit names after creation we need to bring up the **Scene** tab on the Workspace panel and then navigate the tree view, right-click on an object to rename it. Objects must be selected first.

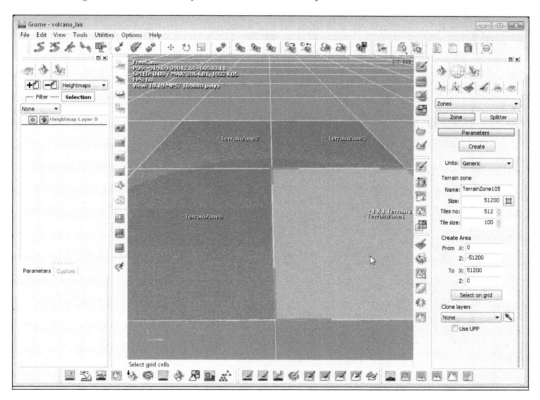

At this point, we have four zones containing a heightmap with a resolution of 512 x 512. As we're going to have the player mostly walking around the interior of the island, we want to increase the ground detail just around the central region which is where we will place our island. There is a really nice shortcut for increasing the mesh resolution in heightmap modifiers (it's called Resample). However, we first need to add more zones in the middle. We could have created more zones initially but we'll assume for the purposes of this exercise that it never hurts to practice adding and removing zones.

To fix our map we're going to split existing zones to make new zones in the center. Then we'll delete the interior ones and rebuild them with twice as many tiles (1024). It's a very simple process.

Splitting zones

With all of the zones selected click on the **Splitter** button. Set the **Split factor** to **2** and click on **Apply** (this will deselect everything, so reselect with *Ctrl + A* to see what happened to our zones). We should see something similar to the following screenshot. Zones are now in a 4 x 4 arrangement.

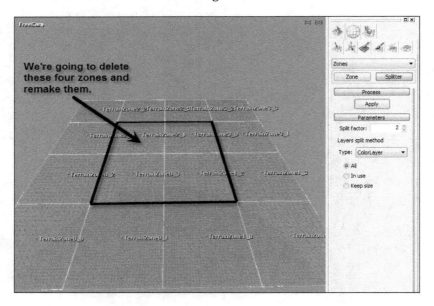

After splitting the zones we will be left with four new zones in the middle. What we're going to do here is select the inner four zones and delete them.

1. Deselect everything (*Ctrl + D*).

2. While holding down the *Ctrl* key either use the mouse to marquee the inner quad or single click on each one. Press the *Delete* key to remove them.

3. Activate the zone creation button and markup the empty quad. Set the value of **Tiles no** to **1024** and click on **Create**.

The following screenshot shows what it should look like once we have selected the four interior zones:

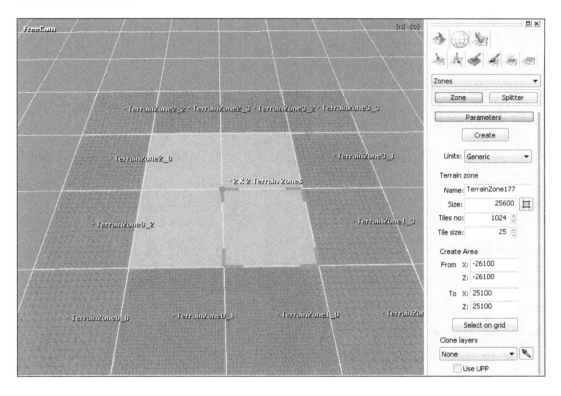

The newly created zones should have twice the ground resolution, being a factor of two larger than surrounding zones.

Hot keys won't work if an edit box has focus. A Viewport must be active for hot keys to function.

If we move the camera closer to the border of zones of differing resolutions it might look like the next screenshot:

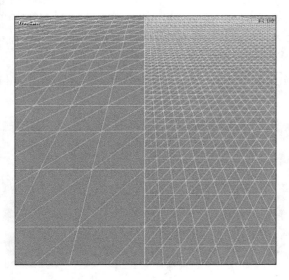

If you have problems seeing the wireframe details you can adjust the LOD range by pressing the comma (,) and period (.) keys to reduce and increase the terrain LOD level respectively.

Now we're ready to start building some detail. Before we launch into the mind boggling possibilities of what GROME can do, let us save our project (*Ctrl + S* to save, or use the **File** menu) and quickly try out some procedural terrain functions.

Creating a simple procedural heightmap

1. In the Tool panel, select the **Modifiers** icon (second icon, second row).
2. Change the drop-down box from **Heightmap** to **Procedural Heightmap**.
3. Select the **FractalNoise** function and the roll-out will display all the available parameters; we'll test one of the presets.
4. Select **Eroded Mountains 3**.
5. Set the **Altitude Range Max** value to **500** and **World Transform Size** to **5120**
6. Click on the **Apply** button.

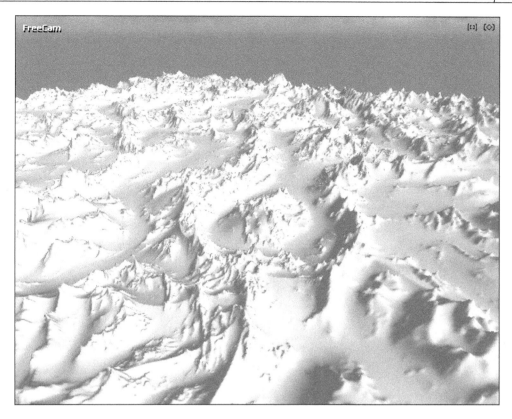

We should end up with a scene similar to this one. Not bad for one modifier but as they say in the music business, it needs more cowbell (in reference to a famous Saturday Night Live TV sketch). To get the best results, we're going to use a combination of several filters and a mask to create our volcanic island paradise. You can walk around it using "Walkcam" (press O or use the Viewport mode to switch). When using a unit size of 1 unit per meter be sure to set the Walking Height to 2.0 meters in the **Workspace/Scene** tab, under **Camera settings**.

Summary

In this chapter, we explored the main areas of the interface, the layer-stack and Tool panel. We went through the functions for creating zones including splitting, modifying, using layers and started work on a map for a video game based on an island. In the next chapter, we will look at the heightmap toolset using brushes and procedural functions.

3
Heightmaps

In GROME, scenes are created using combinations of fractal filters, fluid erosion, and hands-on brushing. Making natural looking terrains is easier in Version 3.1 thanks to the addition of flowmaps which simulate nature's process of water erosion. Heightmaps are edited from the **Tools** panel on the right-hand side via the Modifiers tab.

Modifier toolsets

The drop-down box directly under the Modifier tab selects between three toolsets: **Heightmap**, **Heightmap Brushes**, and **Procedural Heightmap**. We won't go over every tool in detail but instead present a summary of what is available and focus on how some of them can be applied to level design.

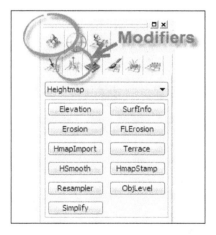

Some of these tools are duplicated for the Heightmap Brush, the only difference being the control of the area and brush shape.

Heightmap toolset

These operations work across selected zones. The sort of things you can do here includes:

- Import a heightmap to a specific location
- Set elevation to an absolute value, or scale it
- Apply surface steps or bevels with a Terrace filter
- Smooth out noise
- Increase or decrease terrain resolution
- Generate a 3D model of terrain for use in mobile platforms
- Flatten terrain to fit under placed 3D objects
- HmapStamp tool is a clone tool that lets you copy one area to another

Elevation

This handy function uniformly sets the terrain height to the specified value. Only selected areas (of armed layers) are modified. In a game, sea-level might be represented by a value of zero which keeps things simple. If we create a mask for rivers and tributaries we can level all water features to the same height and use a simple water plane.

The Elevation tool has four mathematical operations (which are also available to the Brush version of this tool):

- **Raise**: Incrementally increases the value by specified amount
- **Lower**: Reduces the heightmap by the value
- **Level**: Write an absolute height value (useful for sea-levels or plateaus)
- **Scale**: Multiplies the value (below 1.0 reduces, greater than 1.0 increases)

The elevation rollup can be seen in the following screenshot:

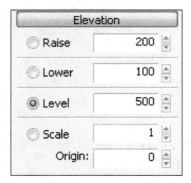

Whatever operation is being performed, the base level is rendered in the viewport as a dark blue rectangle. A light blue rectangle represents the magnitude of the operation. You can click and drag the light blue area to set the value of the operation if you prefer to work by eye (this does not work for the scale operation).

SurfInfo

This is just a handy gizmo that displays world coordinates and height value under the cursor.

Erosion and FLErosion

The difference between these two is quite stark; erosion weathers terrain through a simulated ageing process, taking material from the top of hills and depositing it at the bottom. This has a rounding off effect and some of the pre-sets are good for cliff-face details. When creating terrain and deciding on what filters to use, think about how geological processes would shape real terrain. When experimenting with the Erosion tools it's good practice to test them first on a single zone. Start with a small number of "iterations" in the parameter box (1 to 5). A large number of iterations can take a very long time to process; this is the number of times the algorithm is repeated for the effect.

FLErosion refers to FlowMap Erosion. This simulates water erosion, carving water channels features into terrain. Experimentation is needed to get good results, as always, start with a small number of iterations while you experiment with parameters. The following screenshot shows the result of FLErosion applied to a basic fractal mountain terrain. When combined with FlowMap texturing the results look natural. Best results are obtained with high terrain resolutions which allow for fine details in the FlowMap. For first person shooter type games anything with a 1 meter resolution will be just enough to provide the player some natural cover. Usually the artist will want to apply rocks or other washout debris in these areas. FlowMaps can help here too with procedural placement of such detail objects which we'll look at in *Chapter 5, Bring Me a Shrubbery* which covers detailing.

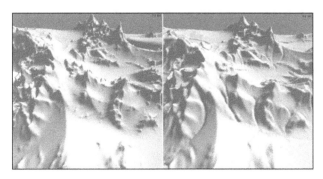

HmapImport

This is a very handy method for stamping a heightmap file from a TGA source into a specific world location. The **World Transform** properties in the rollup sets the scale and origin of the source image (in world units, the image will be centered at the mid-point). If you need coordinates you have two options. Either use the **SurfInfo** tool or go to the **Utilities** menu and choose **Scene Statistics**, the latter displays the center coordinates of the selected region. You can simply paste the coordinates into the X and Z property values (Y is the height value and can be ignored).

Resampler

This is a handy tool which adjusts the resolution of the selected terrain zones. Border zones or areas under the sea can get by with very low resolutions of 64 x 64. Word of warning though, once you reduce the terrain resolution, any fine detail will be lost even if you increase the resolution again.

HSmooth

This applies a simple smoothing operation to the selected zones. If you've tried a procedural function and it appears noisy, this can take the edge off it but it's better to use the Erosion tools if you can.

HmapStamp

This is a clone and stamp tool, great for copying interesting features in your terrain from one area to another. Quickly lasso the feature with the mouse, select the **Transform** radio button, wait a few seconds for the mesh gizmo to be generated and you can drag the gizmo around to where you want, adjust the blending (**Feather**), and click on **Apply** to complete the operation.

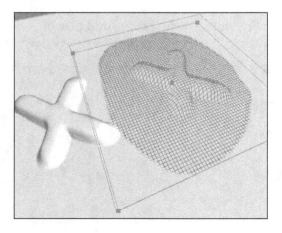

This powerful tool enables us to blend interesting features together or apply simple transformation (such as a scale or rotation) to an existing area of the map. Additionally, we can save out these selections to a disk library for use in other scenes using the **Save** and **Load** buttons.

ObjLevel

This requires an object instance layer (large number of 3D objects scattered across the terrain for example, trees or rocks) and will attempt to level the terrain under every object.

Simplify

This command generates irregular 3D meshes from terrain heightmaps which is useful for devices or engines that do not natively support heightmaps for terrain. For this operation to work, a Mesh layer must be armed and assigned to the current selection. Meshes are exported in Collada DAE format as individual zones. Multiple layers can be created for each LOD stage if we need an LOD mesh for terrain. By reducing the vertex count for each layer, we have precise control over the detail.

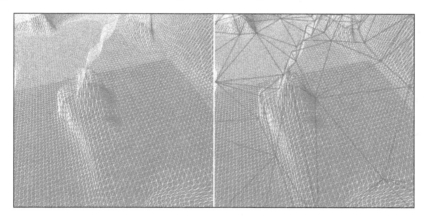

Heightmap Brush toolset

This toolset contains functions applied using a brush. The collection is a mix of functions from the first Heightmap toolset and the Procedural toolset. The difference being that instead of the function being applied to the whole zone, it's applied to the area defined by the shape of the brush.

The brush can either use a circular shape or you can assign a grayscale image as a mask, GROME comes with a set of interesting brushes you can use to add surface texture.

All brush operations use a circular red and green gizmo to indicate the size of the drawing area. The outermost red circle represents the diameter. Brush strokes are applied as a gradient from green to red if any smoothing is in use.

Brush size
Use the square bracket keys (*[* and *]*) to quickly adjust the brush size.

Elevation

Identical to the zone-wide Elevation tool except the rollup contains brush-specific options.

Smudge

The Smudge tool (despite the name) is incredibly useful for game maps. It works like the Heightmap tool's **Level** operation except the height value isn't absolute, it comes from the underlying terrain. Use this tool to paint paths and roads directly onto the surface.

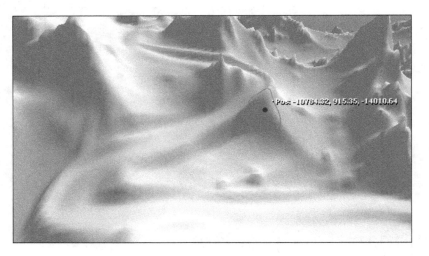

Smooth

Like the Heightmap smooth function with brush parameters. This is more flexible as the brush gives you control over strength.

Clone

The Clone brush gizmo works a little differently than the other brushes. The green circle indicates the clone source of the operation.

[Press and hold down the *ALT* key to define the source location.]

The Clone mode has two important options: Origin and Relative. If the mode is set to Origin, the read position is *reset* after every brush stroke. This allows you to paint multiple copies of the same spot as multiple brush strokes.

If the Relative mode is used, the source cursor simply maintains a relative offset from your brush regardless of how many brush strokes used.

Fractals, hills, mountains, and dunes

These apply their respective procedural functions to the area of the brush. Use them to paint fractals onto sides of a cliff or add interesting surface features. The normals of such details can be baked into a bump map texture to bring them out.

Procedural Heightmap toolset

Procedural functions write to heightmaps of selected zones using fractal algorithms. Some great presets are built into GROME that give some good base layers for a variety of terrain.

PDeposition

This is used to simulate soil deposits, "particles" are dropped at random points. The number of points is set by the **Drop Points** parameter.

FractalNoise and FractalDunes

FractalNoise comes with many pre-sets for a variety of terrain. For any of these pre-sets you should set the Altitude Range parameters to suit the scale of your zone. A min of 0 and max of 1000 clamps the generated terrain features between these values (in world units).

In the following screenshot on the left-hand side we have an example of the Eroded Mountains tool and on the right-hand side Fractal Dunes.

Another value that has a major effect is the World Transform Size parameter, increasing this reduces the density of the fractal noise. Likewise a smaller value increases the density.

The "Method" combo control changes the function used by the fractal generator producing powdery, sharp, basin, or mountains like structures. Experiment with the pre-sets but take care with the altitude ranges.

Usually applying several filters and combining them on the stack allows us to create projects we can quickly test and change. By using the stack to retain overall shapes we can apply more detail to additional layers.

Example – the Heightmap layer stack

We can make use of the Heightmap layer stack to composite different effects, adding Fractal Mountains to one layer, hand painting a river basin in another. For Volcano Island we can add the signature volcano to a separate layer and keep it separate.

To illustrate how these layers interact here's a quick exercise:

1. Start with an empty project and a single zone. Make a total of three Heightmap layers in the layer stack.

2. Assign the selected zone to each of the three layers by right-clicking on each layer and choosing **Assign to selection**.

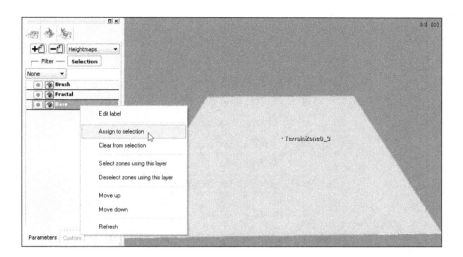

Rename the layers by right-clicking and choosing **Edit label**. Name each layer something like the following:

- Base (will contain our empty heightmap)
- Fractal (contains procedural content)
- Brush (hand-painted elements)

Now make sure that only the top layer **Brush** is "armed" for drawing because we're going to use a Heightmap Brush to paint directly onto the zone. If we had all three with red-dot arm icons then our brush would write to all of them.

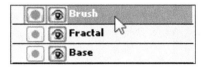

Moving over to the tools panel on the right-hand side; bring up the Modifiers tab for the Heightmap tools and choose **Heightmap Brushes** from the drop-down box. This shows all the functions available for use with brushing. Choose **Elevation** and the appropriate rollup will appear as shown in the following screenshot:

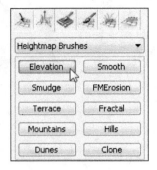

> **Rollup panels**
>
> It can be awkward if you have to repeatedly scroll up and down rollups to change settings. You can drag scroll the panel by holding down the mouse button wherever the mouse pointer changes to a hand.

We'll go over brush functions in a little more detail but for now we'll set the brush diameter (named "Aspect Size") to something about two to three times the value of the zone's **Tiles no**. The size is given in world units.

Set the **Elevation** mode to **Level** and a value of **500**. You might want to check if the **Units** value is set to **100** (this is the "flow" of the brush). A red circle around the mouse cursor indicates the diameter of the operation. When everything looks good you can paint the most hideous phrase ever ushered into programming text books everywhere.

Toggle the Visibility icon on the Brush layer a few times to show and hide our handy-work. Disarm the Brush layer and Arm the Fractal Layer. Change the Modifiers drop-down box to **Procedural Heightmap** and click on **FractalNoise**.

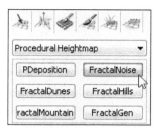

The rollup for this function has many options, we'll use one of the presets, choose Eroded Mountains 3. Change the Altitude Range min value to 0 and max value to 2,000. Click on the **Apply** button. Toggle layer visibility and see how they combine. The height of the brush layer is merged with the fractal layer.

The following four screenshots show individual layers (going clockwise from the top-left); Base, Brush, Fractal, and the final layer is all three combined.

Arm the Brush layer but check all layers are visible (with the little eye button). At the bottom of the Elevation rollup is a section labeled **Surface Options**. This determines the source value of the brush operation. If **Surface** is selected the source value comes from the combined layer stack result, if **Layer** is selected the source value is the active layer.

Heightmap layer operations

A number of useful operations are available when the Selection button is active (click to toggle the **Selection** mode). You must have something selected for this to work, a small + will appear to indicate you can navigate the selection.

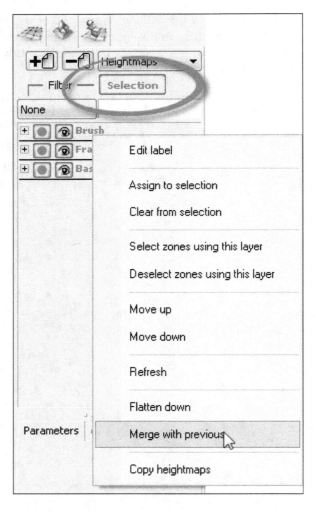

Merging a heightmap

If we need to blend multiple layers together we can merge them together using a layer operation. **Merge with previous** will blend the layer you right-clicked on with the one directly below it.

Flatten down

This merges the combined result of the stack down into the bottom-most layer and removes all heightmap data except for the bottom layer.

Selection masks

GROME provides powerful masking tools commonly found in art applications. In the Workspace panel find the layer stack mode's drop-down list; from here choose **Selection Masks**. Clicking on the "plus page" button adds a new mask layer.

As always we *must* assign a zone to the layer before we can do anything with it, so make a zone active (press *Ctrl* and click on the viewport) and right-click on the layer and **Assign to selection**.

The mask layers needs to be *armed* for use. Any masked areas will show by default as a red tinted area.

Once we have a layer for a mask we usually want to put something in it. The **Tools** panel has a **Selection** tab containing all the tools for creating a mask. A drop-down control under the tab helps choose between Brush and Procedural tools. The interface is nice and consistent in this manner.

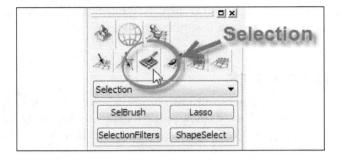

The brush-based selection tools provide methods for painting masks directly onto terrain. As with other brush tools the square bracket keys are handy shortcuts for changing brush diameter.

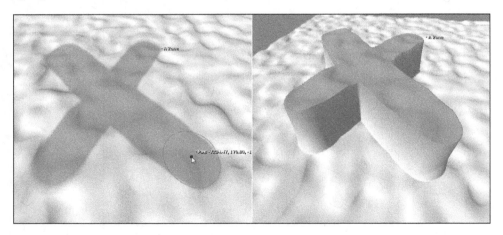

The preceding screenshot shows an "X" painted on a mask layer using the **SelBrush** tool. The image to the right-hand side shows the result of setting the level of the entire heightmap to 1,000 units. Only the terrain under the mask is altered. For an island we could draw or trace the outline onto a mask.

The **Lasso** method is selection by polygon; you draw a shape which completes when you release the mouse button. By default no hot keys are assigned to Select and Deselect modes, you can customize the keyboard command for this.

SelectionFilters are a collection of operations that adjust the internal mask image, these include blur, invert, expand, and shrink. There's some control over contrast and brightness of the mask. Use the Blur operation to create smooth outlines for the mask; we can use this method to create a gentle slope for a beach.

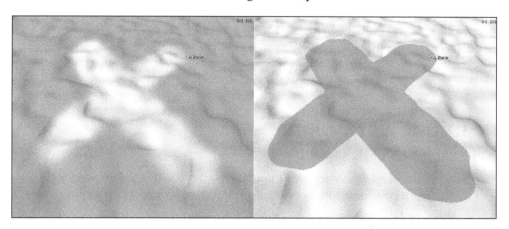

The **ShapeSelect** tool requires a correctly formatted "ESRI" Shapefile which are typically geo-referenced files of roads, waterways, or other real-world map data. If you are modeling real-world areas and need to accurately import geographical features, this tool provides the facility for creating masks for them.

You can obtain ESRI (.SHP) data from a number of sources. The OpenStreetMap is a good starting point as you can download the whole earth in a variety of projections from `http://openstreetmapdata.com/data/land-polygons`.

A white paper describing the file format can be located at `http://www.esri.com/library/whitepapers/pdfs/shapefile.pdf`.

The final toolset for selection masks are procedural – **SelectionGen** and **FlowmapSelect**. SelectionGen is another one of the really handy GROME tools. It performs selection based on an altitude range, slope, and direction.

The final function is FlowmapSelect which will generate a mask that fits the water channel network for your active zones. The Scale parameter adjusts the width of the selection.

View Switching

Sometimes it's better to get a pilot's-eye view when creating or tracing features. Switch the viewport mode to the "Top-down" mode by pressing *T* and zoom the camera out to fit your selection by pressing *Z*.

Return to Freecam mode with the *P* key.

Example – putting it together

Now we've looked at all the pieces we need to create the terrain for our Dr. Yes game project. There's many ways we could approach this but as game developers are keen to say, "There are many ways to skin a cat, but you only get to pick one".

Our initial work plan

Let's draw up a work plan for our proposed map:

1. The island positioned around the map center, the terrain resolution is set to 1,024 (for a production map we might increase this to 2,048 or even 4,096 but this will take longer to work with).

2. Create a mask for the island.

3. Apply heightmap fractals to one layer, then use a brush to bring out island features we want to enhance.

4. Create masks for rivers and elevated areas.

5. Finally, we'll add natural features such as flowmaps and ground noise to the top of the layer stack. We do this in case we make changes lower down.

Let's start by creating two mask layers on our workspace panel. We'll call one "Island" and the other "Rivers". To aid drawing we'll change the color of the River mask to blue by clicking on the colored square and using the color picker.

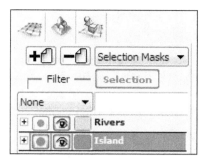

Select and assign four center zones of our map to *both* layers. Arm the "Island" layer and using the Lasso tool trace out an island shape. Arm the River mask and with the brush tool draw a couple of rivers. Arm the Island mask again as we're going to modify it.

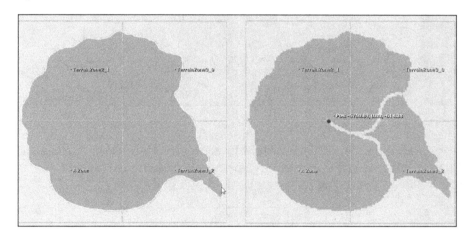

We'll want a smooth transition from ocean to shoreline, using the Blur tool in SelectionFilters repeatedly until we smooth out the coastline enough will do.

Now we're going to add several heightmaps and assign them names:

- RiverMap
- FractalMountains
- IslandBase

Assign the four center zones to each of these layers (as usual; right-click on each layer and click on **Assign to selection**).

Starting with IslandBase, this is our beach and foundation area. Making sure our Island selection mask is active we'll use the Heightmap Elevation tool to set the height to 100 units. The blur on the mask should create a sloped beach as in the following screenshot.

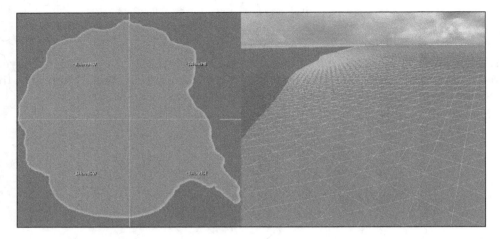

Arm the FractalMountains layer. Now comes a fiddly bit, because we want to use some erosion on the map, GROMEs Fluid Erosion filter doesn't work too well with a lot of flat terrain (for example the sea-bed). So we're going to disarm the mask and fill the entire area with fractal topology then apply Fluid Erosion.

We're using just two fractal pre-sets on this layer, but we'll adjust a couple of the parameters to match our terrain scale:

- **Strange Hills**: Max: 2000, World Transform Size: 10,000
- **Eroded Mountain Noise**: Max: 2000, World Transform Size: 12000

The result might look like the following figure. Feel free to experiment. Because this is supposedly a volcanic island an uneven base (magma pillows) with added mountain topology seemed like a reasonable choice. Jagged rocks are quite young geologically not having time to be weathered.

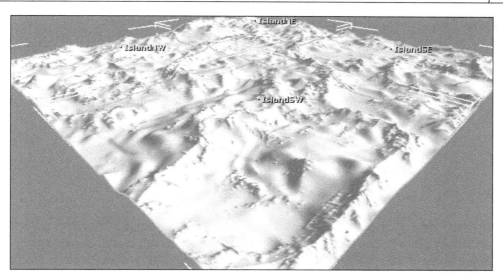

We'll add some soft soil erosion with FLErosion (Heightmap tool), starting with the Power Flow pre-set we'll modify the Smooth rate to 0.1 and Iterations to 5. This might take a few minutes to process. You might want to try and add more weathering effects at this point.

Now to turn it back into an island; arm the Island mask and using SelectionFilters' Invert tool fix the mask so only the ocean is selected. Set the elevation of the sea bed to zero using the Heightmap tool.

In the following screenshot we invert the Island mask (on the left-hand side) then set the ocean area to zero (right-hand side).

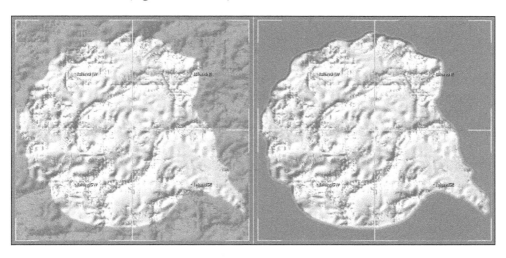

Now to apply the River feature

With only the River mask and the heightmap named "RiverMap" armed, we'll use the Elevation tool to set the height level to zero. Before you do this however we must make sure to check **Surface** in **SurfaceOptions** (Elevation tool). That tells the tool to use the combined surface result for the calculation and not its own layer.

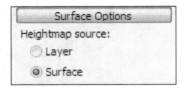

Because the river is applied to the map as a modifier, if you use a brush on the River to set the elevation to zero, you have in effect a history brush tool as writing zero to the River layer erases the modifier and restores the original terrain. Use a smooth brush to even out areas of the river.

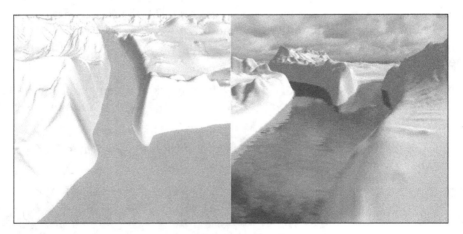

We can use a similar process to add elevation features and our Volcano centerpiece. It's possible the art department might want to create the volcano as a 3D model so we can leave it off the map, but add a place-holder heightmap for it which doesn't disturb our sculpted terrain.

Brushing the shoreline

To finish off our island, we should use a Brush tool with a low strength and high smoothing value to set the level to zero around the shoreline, rounding off cliffs and forming beach areas.

Since we will need to edit the river areas too it's a good idea to arm both the RiverMap and **FractalMountain** layer (and again check the **Surface Options** is set to **Surface**).

Summary

Once we're happy with the overall shape of the island we'll start applying the many texture layers. This is the subject of the next chapter and time to start thinking more about the technical capabilities of our destination game engines. In this chapter, we looked at heightmaps and the wide range of tools in GROME. We looked at how layers interact and modify each other then we went through the creation of selection masks and tools.

Textures and Lighting

4

What's the greatest thing about standards? Well, there are so many to choose from. Game engines such as Unity3D, UDK, Ogre3D, and so on, all load textures for materials. A material is like a cooking recipe, it has a bunch of ingredients (textures) and instructions on how to mix them together. The problem is that there isn't any standard for exchanging materials between these engines or GROME. Some assembly is required.

The GROME exporter will save each of its material layers for every zone. This is potentially quite a large number of files if we get out of control with the number of layers we use. For that reason it's sensible to think about how we can combine layers and how we're going to deal with things like noise textures in the host engine.

Ogre3D is an open source and extensible rendering engine. Of the engines we'll be looking at in this book it's the only one that has a terrain plugin natively using GROME's Graphite engine. Scene composition and rendering will closely match that of the editor. Whatever engine is used, we can squeeze out more visual quality through post-processing and production quality textures.

For the purpose of this book we are restricted to using stock GROME textures, however all licensed users can download additional textures and content packs from Quad Software. You can use your own textures easily enough (the built-in package browser lets you add your own library locations).

Performance consideration for mobiles

Unity3D on mobile platforms such as iPhone and Android will likely require shadows and lightmaps baked into the terrain textures. Real-time lighting and shadows on terrain objects is simply too costly in terms of performance. All texture layers should be merged into a single layer for these platforms. This is done using the ColorBake tool which we'll look at in this chapter.

Working with material layers

The workspace panel, once again, has a layer stack for working with textures called **Materials**. Similar to other modes we need an active layer for our tools to work.

So before we can work with textures we must have at least one material layer armed, and have a zone assigned to that layer. Go ahead and create a couple of material layers; call them Beach, Plains, and Mountains.

Terrain textures are rendered as layers in the order they sit on the stack. The top-most layer being rendered last.

Assigning zones to a layer

As with heightmaps we assign zones to a layer by right-clicking on the layer and selecting the **Assign to selection**. For material layers a dialog box appears asking for texture information.

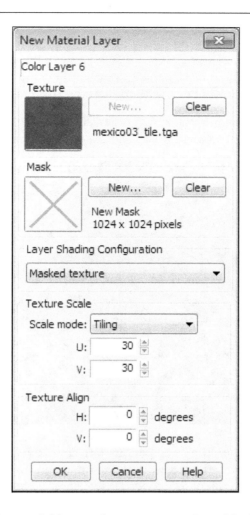

There are two types of material layers, how you populate this dialog will determine the layer type. A material can be a simple color layer (a texture stretched over the terrain surface) or a masked texture.

Color textures

A color texture allows us to add a texture (such as a satellite image) to a zone but more importantly they allow us to paint color directly using the ColorBrush tool. This give the artist full control over feathering and shading effects.

Color textures really come into their own when combined with other layers to create tonal variations across a landscape on a zone-by-zone basis.

In the preceding screenshot, the image on the left-hand side is our example island terrain with multiple texture layers added. The image on the right-hand side has an additional simple color layer assigned. This is a simple texture added for tonal variation. By setting the material blend mode to **Color Add** (blend modes in GROME are referred to as "Shader configuration") the color from the texture is blended.

Each zone in the layer can have its own texture and blend mode by activating the layer stack **Selected** button and expanding the tree. Clicking on the texture assigned to each zone allows you to individually select the image file you want.

Ground holes

Color layers are useful for creating a special mask that hides selective areas of the terrain. When a layer uses the "Ground Holes" Shader configuration, black pixels in the color texture will appear invisible (although the geometry is still present).

This image shows a chequered board color texture using the Ground Hole shader. To work correctly the layer should be at the bottom of the stack (first rendered). This can be useful for embedding caves and basements which are 3D objects that are often embedded into terrain.

By masking the terrain this way, it won't visually intersect with internal building spaces. Players might feel disturbed when entering a building only to pass through the ground on their way to the cellar.

Masked textures

We mentioned masked textures earlier, most of the texture tools deal with modifying masks. Simply put, a masked texture type gives us the means to selectively paint textures inside a zone.

By mixing different layers we create textures that match the topography of the landscape, one layer for grass, one for rock, one for cliff faces, one for snow, and so on. It's important to grasp that when you have a masked texture layer and you use a tool to paint it, what you're actually doing is painting the mask which controls visibility of the texture.

Black values in the mask equals no texture; white areas of the mask represent full intensity. Like heightmaps, pixel intensity determines the end value.

When we use brushes or procedural functions to apply textures these operations are simply writing intensity values into the mask. This is similar to the technique known as "Splatting" used in some game engines.

To create a mask, first we can click on the empty image box in the mask selector (when empty, this has a large "X" through it). We can then select an image to use as a mask. Moreover, we can create a new mask by clicking on the **NEW** button. This brings up a **New Image** dialog (shown next).

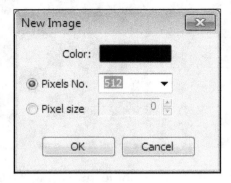

This dialog sets the resolution and initial color value written into the generated mask. If you need to set the mask so the texture is fully visible after creation, change the color to solid white (clicking on the color box brings up a standard color picker).

The texture toolset

The fourth tab on the tools panel brings up the texturing features. The drop-down control allows us to select between the brush, procedural, and decal tools.

ColorGen tool

This tool requires an active color texture and paints areas that match specified terrain parameters (altitude range, slope, orientation) with a color.

It does this using a component you'll see in several of the texture tools, called a **Distribution Mask (DM)**, these are found in the rollup of the ColorGen and MaskGen tools. They tell the editor how we want to apply a color or texture to a terrain based on a set of parameters. The tools can use one or more DMs and process them in a single operation although they can be fiddly to work with and often it's easier to use one at a time on different layers. Let's look at a single Distribution Mask component, refer back to this section if you need a reminder.

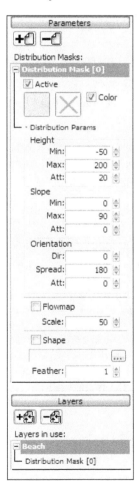

Distribution Mask component

The plus and minus icons at the top will add and remove Distribution Masks. The default name will have the count in square brackets (for example, **Distribution Mask [0]**).

 It's possible to right-click on the Distribution Mask name to enter a more user friendly one.

Importantly, clicking on the name area of the Distribution Mask toggles its use. This is the mechanism by which the Distribution Masks are added to the **Layers in use** list, at the very bottom of the rollup.

The **Active** checkbox is a quick means of toggling the Distribution Mask, we might have several in a preset but only want to use one.

The color picker box chooses how the material will be painted. If we want a texture instead, uncheck the **Color** box and click on the "X" box to pick a texture from the package browser dialog.

Height values should be populated with the altitude range we only want to paint. **Att** is the attenuation (fade) value (inversely proportional to the distance between **Min/Max**). A bigger value will blend the boundary over a larger area.

Slope allows you to specify the min and max angle to paint, a max value of 45 will only paint on surfaces with an angle of up to 45 degrees.

Orientation sets the direction we want to paint and **Spread** is the angle offset left and right, so 180 degrees both left and right would be the full coverage.

The **Flowmap** checkbox will calculate water channels from the terrain surface and write only to these areas, the scale determines how broad the channels are.

To use a shape to define the drawing area you need to have a georeferenced ESRI shape file. Professional mapping tools can import and export these for bodies of water, roads, or anything that you might need in a real map. If we had real-world road data in such a format we could write solid colors or an asphalt texture directly onto the layer.

Layers and Layers in use

Before we can click on the **Apply** button we must add at least one Distribution Mask to the **Layers in use** parameter (this area of the rollup is shown next).

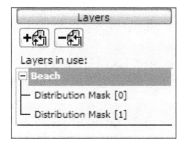

To add a Distribution Mask to the operation we must ensure the following:

- We have a Color layer armed and selected (workspace panel)
- The name of the Distribution Mask is highlighted
- The name of the armed layer is highlighted in the **Layers in use** panel
- We click the "+" icon to add the Distribution Masks

Phew! Seems like a lot of steps. However, once you've had to do it a few times it becomes second nature.

Adding Distribution Masks

When you need to add more than one Distribution Mask, you can hold down the *Ctrl* key to highlight them and click on the "add" icon. Otherwise, you have to add them one at a time.

One thing we must consider, however, is that if we change the topography later then we may need to rebuild the texture layer. Watch out for shadows and cliff faces in particular as these will change if you go back to edit the heightmap.

Shadowmap tool

These bake shadows onto a material layer which is perhaps not desirable if you're designing for a game engine with real-time lighting and shadows (Unity Pro, UDK). Even so, if your game has fixed shadows then baking shadows onto the terrain is a good idea for performance.

Not only does this give you distant shadows, it also adds some depth to a scene. This tool will also generate shadows for 3D objects placed into the scene by GROME using the instance and vegetation tools which we'll cover later.

To create a shadow map we need to use the procedural shadowmap tool on a prepared material layer. For the material layer we need to use a masked texture.

Steps to create a shadowmap layer are given as follows:

- Create a new layer
- Assign zones to the layer
- Select "New" mask; color should be black, set size to desired resolution
- For texture, click on the "X" box to bring up the package browser, navigate to `misc/shadow.tga` and select the black image
- Change the Layer Shadowing Configuration to "Masked Detail"

Once your layer is ready and armed for use, from the procedural shadowmap tool, set the light direction as required (a button labeled **Get Camera Direction** will rotate the light source to match camera rotation).

Click on **Apply** and wait for the operation to complete. This can take a long time if you have many zones or a high resolution shadow map.

The layer should be placed at the top of the layer stack so the terrain shadows are rendered on top of everything else.

If the shadow map reduces the brightness of the scene too much you can tweak the map using the **MaskFilter** tool next to it on the panel. This is shown in the following screenshot. On the left-hand side, the new shadowmap, on the right-hand side, the shadowmap adjusted using the MaskFilter.

Reducing the brightness slightly and increasing the contrast on the mask will lighten the scene and deepen the shadows like bright sunlight. If the map suffers from leopard spots as a result of terrain noise you could try applying a Blur MaskFilter.

If you need to retouch the shadowmap using a brush for whatever reason, set the texture tool mode to **Brushes** and use the **MaskBrush** tool which will allow you to paint shadows directly.

You shouldn't ever need to do this; it's easier to simply rebuild the whole shadowmap.

MaskFilter tool

This has exactly the same controls as the **SelectionFilter** tool. The difference of course is that this tool works on the texture mask. We can **Invert**, **Blur**, **Shrink**, **Expand**, and adjust **Brightness/Contrast**. **Brightness** effectively adjusts mask opacity; a darker mask is more opaque.

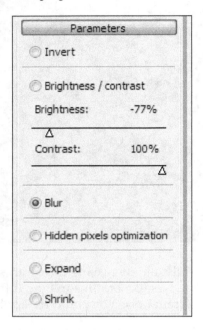

The final operation **Hidden pixel optimization** removes areas of the mask that are hidden by layers above. This is important when exporting masks to other engines where they are combined into a single image and ideally you need a normalized mask.

MaskGen tool

At the heart of this tool and perhaps the most important for dynamically texturing terrain is the Distribution Mask component (see the ColorGen tool for a breakdown if you skipped it). The MaskGen tool operates on masked texture layers and procedurally generates the mask for the layer based on terrain topography as described by a series of Distribution Masks.

The tool comes with a number of useful presets for painting some kinds of terrain and vertical surfaces for mountainous terrain. Let's look at one of those and get an idea of what it does by example.

Bring up the MaskGen tool and from the presets select **AridVegetation**. This has four Distribution Masks which we'll apply to separate material layers. Clear the material stack and we'll create four materials. We'll name them after the Distribution Masks as, Base, 01, 02, and Detail.

For each of these layers we need to assign our four island zones to them and create a new mask. For texture choice we'll pick random ones for now. But the important thing is that we create a mask of at least 1,024 resolution with some texture attached.

The Base layer

Starting with the Base texture layer, arm it and select the Base DM in the MaskGen rollup, add it to **Layers in use**, and apply. The whole of the map should take on that texture's appearance as the Base DM covers pretty much everything.

In the workspace panel, expand the Base material and set the Base texture to use arid/stone/rock06.dds. Set the tiling UV to 20.

The 01 layer

Disarm all layers and arm layer 01. From the MaskGen tool, select the DM also named "01", add it to the **Layers in use** and click on the **Apply** button. This preset is assigned to generate a wide flowmap effect.

To get good contrast from it we should pick a light color texture. Assign the texture to something like Romanian_sand05.dds and the tiling UVs to 100 again. You should see dry riverbed effects on the terrain surface. If not, go back and check everything was selected correctly. It's easy to miss a step but practice makes perfect.

Arm 02 Texture layer

This layer will be used to cover flat plain areas. So we'll pick a suitable desert plains texture from the provided library, satellite/mexico03_tile.tga. As before, disarm all layers then arm layer 02. We're now ready to apply Distribution Mask 02 from the MaskGen rollup.

Assign the layer in use and click on the **Apply** button. Adjust the UVs to 30 (or whatever looks reasonable for the scale of the terrain).

Final Detail layer

The detail layer is a bit different. We'll assign the texture `dry_mud01` and set the UV tiling to `500` each. From the material stack we should change the "Shader Configuration" to "Masked Bright Detail". What this does is, it adds an offset to the color blending so the layer appears brighter.

Select the Detail Distribution Mask, add it to the layer in use (which should be the Detail texture layer) and apply it.

A detail texture appears when viewing the terrain close to ground level, it helps sell the scale of the scene at low level.

All done

By applying variations and experimenting with textures, scales, and blending, it's possible to create seasonal variations from the same scene. You might want to try using the MaskFilters to blur or expand some of the layer coverage, just to get a feel for the different effects.

Ideally you need about eight or nine layers on a map to achieve really good results. Improvements we could make include more rocky details, flowmap enhancements and water features. Our final mask example will cover the creation of cliff faces using vertical mapping.

Vertical texture mapping

This is the process by which we combine two texture layers to correctly map a flat texture to vertical surfaces such as mountains and cliff faces. Some 3D engines can have some kind of vertical mapping built into a pixel shader which is very handy when available. However, we can't always rely on this; for our project we can assume the mobile platforms will require baked textures with correctly mapped vertical surfaces. We can create two layers to achieve accurate vertical mapping in the following manner:

- Create our first material layer for cliffs, we'll name this `Mountains 0-90`.
- Assign it a nice Canyon Rock texture (such as the `arid2/canyon_rock01.tga` texture as provided in the GROME texture library).
- Create a new mask, default values are fine for this example.
- In the parameters for the texture set the UV tiling to something that fits the scene (for example `20, 20`). Set the HV spin for this layer to `0, 90`. This is shown in the following screenshot.

- Now the tricky part, using the **MaskGenerator** tool, find the preset named **Vertical 0 90**.

- With our **Mountains 0-90** layer active, hold down *Ctrl* and press the left mouse button and select the preset mask parameters named **Vertical 0 90 (1)** and **Vertical 0 90 (2)** (shown in the following screenshot on the right-hand side).

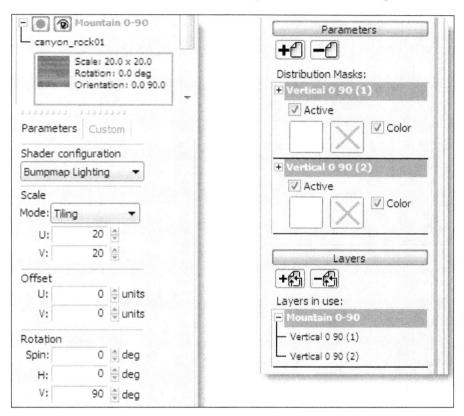

- Click on the **MaskGenerator** tool's **Apply** button to map the texture to the vertical surfaces.

- Now we create the second vertical layer for textures that run perpendicular. Name this layer Mountains 90-90.

- Assign it the same texture (Canyon Rock as before).

- Create a new mask, again with the default values.

- In the parameters for this texture we'll set the same UV tiling values (20, 20). But this time we set the HV spin for the layer to 90, 90.

- With the **MaskGenerator** tool, find the preset named **Vertical 90 90**.

- With the **Mountains 90-90** layer active, hold down *Ctrl* and press the left mouse button and select the preset mask parameters named **Vertical 90 90 (1)** and **Vertical 90 90 (2)** (shown in the following screenshot on the right-hand side). Click the layer's **Add** button.

- Click the **MaskGenerator** tool's **Apply** button to map the texture to the vertical surfaces.

Assuming we got everything correct our vertical surfaces should be suitably mapped by two texture layers as show in the following screenshot:

ColorBake tool

For mobile platforms in particular, baking multiple layers into a single layer has enormous performance benefits. This is different from merging down layers on the layer stack. This method leaves our original source layers intact.

The Color Bake operation combines all visible layers (from top to bottom) into the bottom-most visible layer. By combining our layers into a single layer we have a texture we can export that works great for mobile platforms and overhead maps.

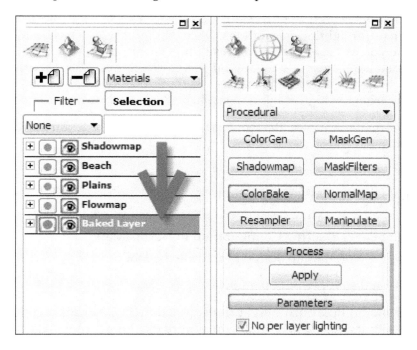

To create a baked layer we create a color texture on the layer stack (assign zones by right-clicking on it, when the new material dialog box appears click on the **New** texture).

The resolution chosen for the color texture will equal the highest resolution the baked texture can carry, it's likely that a loss of detail will occur. For mobile platforms, it's probably not wise to choose anything higher than a resolution of 1,024. If the scene has a detail texture then this will be lost in the bake. Although the detail texture could be reapplied in the host game engine by the programmer, this can be done as part of the engine material definition.

The **No per layer lighting** option should be ticked to discard lighting information from layers during the bake process.

NormalMap tool

A normal map (sometimes referred to as a bump map) can be generated automatically from the currently visible terrain surface. This tool requires a color texture layer to write on. The purpose of a NormalMap is to bake information on surface normals for lighting calculations. Once that information has been baked into a texture you can use much lower resolution terrain surfaces without losing the bumpy details, even at mid to long range view distances. This is ideal for games where we need to use terrain exported as low resolution meshes, we can retain the surface detail from the high-resolution mesh.

To create a normal map using the tool, first create a new color texture layer on the material stack:

- New material layer
- Right-click on **Assign to selection**
- Click on **New** texture (assign resolution to something like 1,024), click on **OK**
- Set the **Layer Shading Configuration** to NormalMap
- Click the NormalMap button to activate the tool
- Click on the **Apply** button and wait

Your terrain should turn purple and green(ish). From the layer stack, drag the layer to the bottom. Toggle its visibility to admire the difference it makes to the scene lighting.

 The normal map format is `RGB = normal.XYZ`, with `normal.X` and `normal.Z` normalized from -1 – 1 to 0 – 1 interval (`normalized = (original + 1) * 0.5`) so they fit into color channel.

`Normal.Y` doesn't need to be normalized, for terrain this normal is always facing up.

Let it snow

For a change of scenery let's add some snow to highland regions. Create a new material layer (we'll call it `SnowField`). Assign the terrain zones to the layer and we'll pick the texture `terrain/cold/snow02.dds`, setting the tiling UVs to `100`. For the mask we'll create a new one with a size of 1,024.

Go to the **MaskGen** tool, pick the preset named **MountainsSnow**. We'll only use one Distribution Mask from this, the one named **Snow** but we'll edit the **Height** settings as thus:

	Height	Slope
Min	1000	0
Max	10000	30
Att	150	5

Assign the Snow Distribution Mask to the **Layers in use** (the material layer called **SnowField** should be armed to appear in the list). Click on the **Apply** button.

The brush tools

The brush tools are near identical to those used for heightmaps and selection masks. The obvious difference is that the ColorBrush tool paints the selected color into the active color layers.

The MaskBrush tool is useful for touching up masked textures. The color value here is a simple intensity slider offering values from 0 to 255. Transparent being 0 and fully opaque being a value of 255.

The package browser

This is a common dialog that typically appears when you select a texture, mask shape, or 3D object. It's simply a tool that presents previews of files contained within installed packages and your own filesystem. It's recommended you make use of the **Favorites** feature when working collaboratively, adding your own files by clicking in the tree and selecting **Add to favorites**.

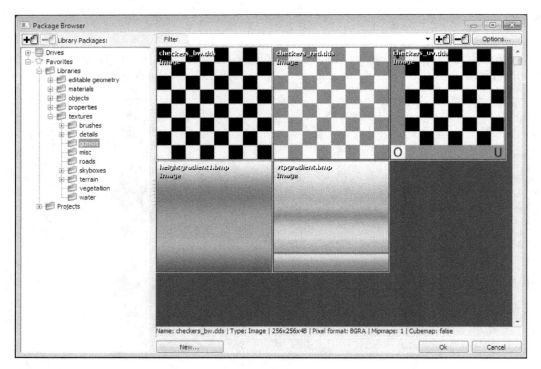

Decals

Apart from painting with textures, GROME can use decals to apply spot graphics such as helipads or scorched earth. **Decals** are individual objects that project images down onto a surface. While individual game engines might support some kind of decal system, they will not translate. It's not possible to bake decal objects into a texture prior to export but as objects they can be exported. However; the onus is on the end user and the host engine to load and handle them. We'll have a quick look at the Decal tool.

Before creating any decals you must (as with all other tools) create a Decal layer on the layer stack then assign at least one terrain zone to the new layer. When you click on **Assign to selection** the **New Decal Layer** dialog appears. This is shown in the following screenshot:

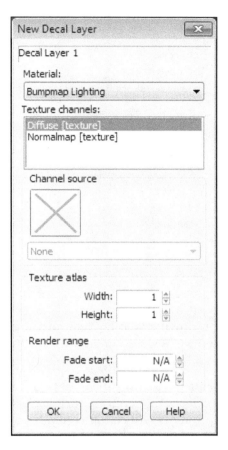

Decals are treated as individual objects you can position with the mouse. They lay flat with the terrain but they are made from triangular meshes that are updated with terrain height information when you edit them. They share the same resolution as the containing zone, consequently having lots of large decals on a high resolution mesh will really eat into you polygon budget. However, they are useful for placing spot effects or serving as markers for spawn points.

Each decal has its own size, rotation, and scale parameters. You edit these by selecting the decal with the Decal tool active and applying the desired values in the tool rollup.

The layer stack panel in Decal mode allows you to set a fade-in and fade-out distance for the decal set.

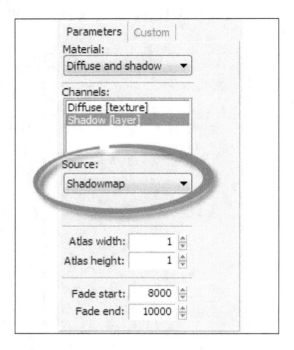

By setting the **Material** drop-down box to **Diffuse and shadow**, you can combine the decal texture with the contents of a shadowmap by selecting the layer in the **Source** drop-down box.

Decals can also use what's called a texture atlas. A texture atlas is simply a single texture file that contains a collection of images, such as sprites or a bitmap font. Somewhere an atlas description file will contain an index and coordinates on the texture for any image contained in the atlas. The most basic form of texture atlas is an evenly spaced grid where each cell contains one image. This is supported by GROME Decals by specifying the **Atlas width** and **Atlas height** properties for an image.

To move decals around, click and drag the large green dot on the selected instance (instances have a red border when selected). To manipulate decals two conditions must be satisfied. First, the decal layer must be armed; secondly a decal tool must be active. All the decals in the layer will have a yellow border when both conditions are met.

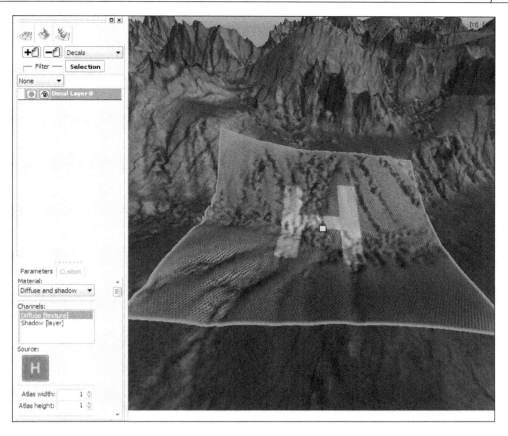

This screenshot shows a decal of an oversized helipad, note the mesh near perfectly matches the uneven water channels of the terrain mesh. Additionally, the **Diffuse and shadow** material is using the shadowmap layer, which is then blended over the top of the decals diffuse texture. How smart is that?

Summary

In this chapter, we looked at the hand brushing, procedural texture tools, how to build a shadow map and bake multiple layers into a single texture. We looked at normal maps, the package browser, and finally the decal tool. In the next chapter, we'll look at vegetation, grass, trees, and detail layers.

5

Bring Me a Shrubbery

Vegetation has a huge impact on scene quality. Significant coverage was once difficult to achieve without making compromises for memory and rendering power. Early computer games would use single pixels to sell the impression of movement (and sometimes even that was a stretch). Thanks to current **Graphics Processing Unit (GPU)** technology it's realistic to have lush scenes consisting of 2,50,000 vegetation objects on mid-range gaming PCs.

GROME, Unity, and other game engines all have their own unique vegetation system but broadly speaking they do the same thing; take a single object (such as a tree or grass billboard) and draw thousands of copies at different locations within the scene.

Games commonly use smoke and mirror techniques to fool the eye into thinking a scene is more complex than it is, even using old cinema tricks like forced perspective. The amount of detail we want to include is impacted by the altitude of the camera in our game; a flying game would require us to have a more distant view. In a first-person walking game we expect to see grasses and plants.

Our goal is to present a reasonably detailed scene from a first person viewpoint which means filling screen real estate (pixels) with enough detail to keep the eye interested.

Some of the tricks used include doubling the scale of vegetation objects to fill more screen area. A shrubbery that's two meters wide becomes four meters wide. Obviously an object twice as large fills twice as much screen area (perspective not withstanding). The more screen you can fill like this means you don't need as many objects. The net result is increased coverage. Games can make use of exaggerated tree scales, larger trunks on smaller numbers of trees will appear denser. By tweaking the scale of an individual object replicated thousands of times, the impression of a dense forest can be had with some simple visual trickery. Quite often the most subtle tweaks for improving the visual footprint of a tree model is thickening up the transparent portions of the textures used on the branches.

As an exercise for the reader, play through a variety of 3D games on a console or PC and see if you can pick out vegetation that doesn't seem to match the scale of the surrounding objects. These visual tricks are not obvious unless you're looking for them, which is true of all the best trickery.

It takes a keen eye and a good deal of experimentation to create suitable assets that greatly contribute to filling an outdoor scene while at the same time keeping rendering performance high.

The genre of the game is an important factor. As touched upon earlier, first person games have a short horizon; it's easy to spot discontinuity of scale but the maximum culling range (the distance at which you stop rendering ground detail from the camera) is quite short. For vehicle games or flying games the problem is one of rendering enough ground cover to represent entire patches of woodland out to long distances down to blades of grass when landing.

For flying-based games, distant ground shadows baked under areas of vegetation really sell the density. Up close, the 3D detail models of trees and grass will cover up any baked shadows and generated shadows will blend in perfectly. This works for first-person games too but can be considered optional. A shadowmap based on vegetation coverage is a good idea anyways, since it can be used to modify the intensity of objects outside of any real-time shadow rendering range.

Exportability of vegetation

Vegetation data does not translate well to Unity and UDK, there's no easy way to move it unless they are using GROME's native Graphite engine (such as the Ogre3D Graphite rendering module).

The most practical method of transferring vegetation coverage to Unity and UDK is through the use of coverage masks. GROME uses masks to populate vegetation within zones and these are saved as image files by several of the built-in exporters.

These masks can (with some effort) be imported into Unity and UDK but this presents practical editing issues should we need to perform any fine-tuning to the game map. Once a bulk transfer of vegetation data has been completed, any edits later on become more difficult to integrate, especially if it's required to reimport everything, potentially losing many hours of work. For this reason I usually recommend using Unity or UDKs built-in vegetation tools from this point onward but there are no hard-and-fast rules.

GROME detail objects and billboards

GROME's vegetation layers have a set of properties controlling visibility range, fade-out distance, and create objects where one model is swapped for a lower detail one (Level of Detail "LOD" collections). It also supports **billboards**; a term used in computer graphics to describe a textured quad that always faces the camera. A billboard quad is aligned to the camera using a vertex shader on the 3D hardware and can process thousands of billboards very quickly. Most game engines support this kind of object.

GROME vegetation layers are named "Detail" layers since it can render any kind of object such as rocks or debris, not just vegetation.

GROME also divides detail layers into two very distinct types:

- 3D Objects
- Billboards

You specify the type of detail layer when assigning zones to a Detail layer. Again these types won't export directly to our game engines.

The Detail layer stack

To set the mode of the layer stack to **Details** we set it from the drop-down control in the workspace panel, as shown in the following screenshot:

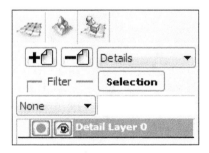

Adding grass billboards

As with all modes of the layer stack, a layer is assigned one or more zones from the scene by right-clicking on a layer and selecting **Assign to selection**. Doing so will present us with a dialog box (shown in the following screenshot) which applies selected detail objects according to a coverage mask (which is empty on creation).

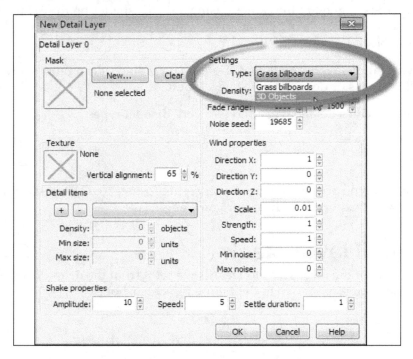

The **Type** drop-down control on the dialog helps to toggle between the two modes; **Grass Billboards** and **3D Objects**. This changes the input parameters on the lower parts of the dialog. Billboards have additional parameters for wind animation.

Grass billboards can make use of strips of images to create variations using a single layer. The GROME texture library contains a selection of these consisting of four types of color matched grass. An example image strip is shown as follows:

The **Texture** settings in the **New Detail Layer** dialog allows us to specify different billboard sizes and density values for each subimage.

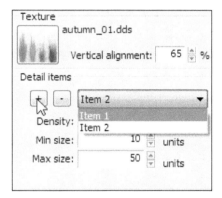

When using an image strip it's important we click the **+** button to correctly set the number of **Detail items** so that it is equal to the number of images in the strip. If we don't, the whole strip will be used for the billboard and the results will look a little strange, especially when the camera is rotated.

Adding 3D Object details

This is accomplished from the same **New Detail Layer** dialog box, however the **Type** drop-down control presents a different set of controls. This is shown in the following screenshot:

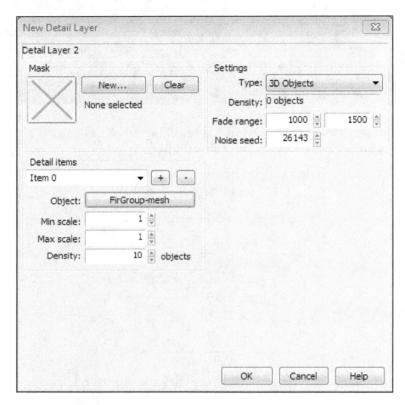

3D Objects should have a small polygon count as many will end up being drawn in the scene. The **Density** value is the maximum number of these objects that will be placed at random (in an algorithm that uses **Noise seed** as a placement modifier) inside each "cell". A cell is a single pixel of the coverage mask. When you create a mask you're asked for resolution (default is 512 x 512 pixels) and a color to initialize the mask with. Remember, white is maximum coverage, black is zero coverage.

This mask will be added to each zone, so it will be stretched to fit. If you need fine control over coverage use a high-resolution mask but it's better to keep it small and adjust the density as required.

The Detail toolset

For creating coverage masks for detail objects we have three kinds of tools: Brushes, Mask import, and Procedural.

Brush tool

The brush tool operates in a similar manner to the Masked Texture brush tool or selection brush tool. You paint a value into the coverage mask and the Graphite engine populates the area according to the layer's parameters.

You can use the brush size hotkeys (square brackets) to adjust coverage as you paint. The tool roll-up has three radio buttons controlling the paint mode. You add, subtract, or write an absolute value to the mask. Setting an absolute level of zero will erase details. The next screenshot shows an example of painting with the brush tool from a top-down camera view.

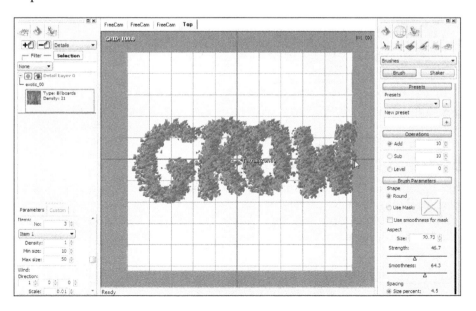

Mask tool

This enables us to import a grayscale image and apply it to a specified area and size. The imported image is positioned such that it is centered at the position indicated by the **Origin** coordinates on the tool panel. To get the coordinates you can use the **Scene Statistics** option in the **Utilities** menu at the top of the window. Assuming you have just the zones you want to cover selected, the center point will be given (you can ignore the Y value). The mask will cover the specified size in world units. An example of applying a mask is shown as follows:

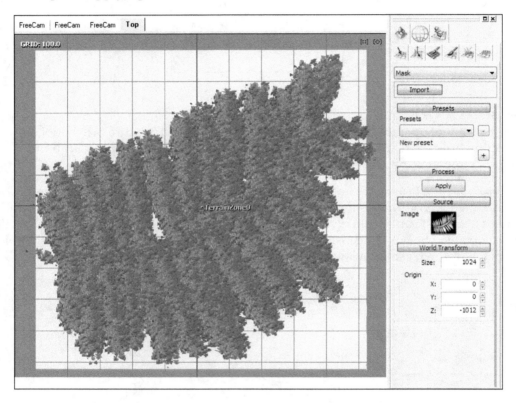

Procedural tools

Two tools are listed in the procedural toolset: Generator and Resampler. The Resampler tool allows us to adjust the resolution of the coverage mask. Simply set the new resolution and click on the **Apply** button (as with all tools you need a selection and the layer should be armed for use otherwise no operation can take place).

The Generator is the most fun and time saving tool of the collection. It operates on the same principles as Masked Textures. Using one or more Distribution Masks it will apply values to the coverage mask according to the parameters specified in each DM parameter. Each Distribution Mask specifies information about altitude range, slope angle, and orientation. Using these we apply details to specific areas of terrain topography. Grasses on plains, rocks on hills, and trees placed below fixed altitudes. It's capable of doing a lot a work for the artist. Applying many layers of vegetation detail is a time-consuming task in some game engines; large game worlds are especially challenging.

A quick example

Starting with an empty project we will make a single zone and apply a procedural heightmap operation to give it some features (making the altitude range something like 0 to 200 units). Just so we have a simple heightmap, or paint some features using a brush.

Let's walk through the steps to create a single grass layer:

1. Add a detail layer to the layer stack and assign it to the zone. When the new detail dialog appears set the type to **Grass Billboards**.

2. Click on the **New...** mask button (keeping the default values) and pick a grass texture from the GROME library.

3. Using the Procedural Generator tool we're going to map the grass to the height range 0 to 100 and avoid slopes greater than 20 degrees.

4. Filling out the Distribution Mask as shown previously and adding it to the **Layer in use** at the bottom of the roll-up.

5. Add a small value to the **Att** (attenuation) field to feather the detail.

6. Make sure the Apply method is set to **Replace**.

7. Click on the **Apply** button.

The result should approximate the following screenshot:

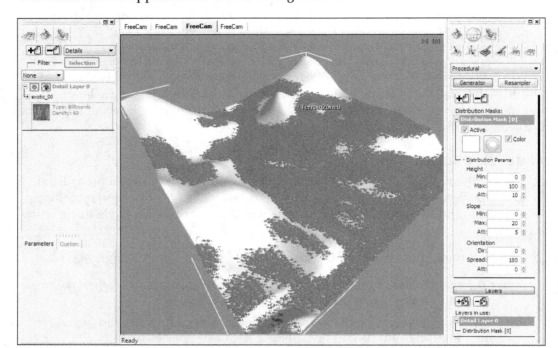

Experiment with different ranges and "color" value in the Distribution Mask. Note how different shades of gray alter the density of the detail coverage.

A closer look at Billboard Grasses

GROME like other game engines creates a "moving carpet" of grass detail centered on the camera. As the player moves, any grass object moving out of range disappears. New grass objects are faded into view in front of the player. Quite often this moving carpet is noticeable in games but careful attention to match the color between the grass and terrain textures can greatly reduce the visual impact of the pop-in effect.

When adding grass or any detail layer we should take time to set the fade start and fade end parameters. This sets the size of this "moving carpet" in which the billboards are visible.

To make things interesting, the Graphite engine used by GROME does a pretty good job of blending **material** layers with **detail** layers to blend baked shadows with dynamic lighting. This is similar to how decals can have an optional material layer applied during rendering. For Unity and UDK we don't need to concern ourselves with these options, they have their own methods for doing this kind of blending.

Blending shadowmaps with vegetation

If we have created a material layer containing a baked shadowmap, we can use this to neatly blend grass billboards with the shadowmap as illustrated in the following screenshot. This greatly improves the scene at little cost.

You can find this setting below the detail layer stack when you have expanded and selected the layer (see the following dialog image).

Here we have in our scene a material layer simply named **Shadowmap** containing baked shadows. From the Detail layer parameters, we simply select the material layer we want to use for **Shadow**.

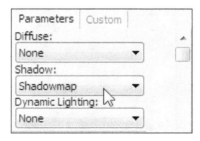

Also note that we can set layers that modify the diffuse color and lighting of vegetation. This is handy for providing more natural color blending in GROME but not widely supported in other engines.

3D Objects in detail layers

The Detail tools, when using a layer set to 3D Object types, are identical to using grass billboards except in place of quads the engine will use a DAE (Collada) object. When you consider that many thousands of these might be generated in a small space it's recommend you test small sample areas or use the hand brushing tools.

There's one caveat to using Detail layers for large objects such as trees; they don't cast any shadows. The shadowmap texture tool doesn't create shadows for 3D Objects placed in this manner. If we wish to hand-place trees it's a good idea to use the Object tools (on an Object layer) which is for placement of 3D entities. Forests and trees placed using this method will have shadows baked by the shadowmap tool, as shown in the following screenshot:

Exporting vegetation as instanced objects results in a text file containing coordinate sets, not an image map. A special importer will be required to pull this data into our game. Another point to consider is that the host engine might render objects differently, therefore baked shadows won't match.

Unity 3D can render and bake vegetation shadows onto terrains so that you can skip this process altogether.

One final point about masks; during the GROME export process, every layer for each stack and each zone is exported as a mask. The exported masks are in a common image format (BMP, PNG, DDS, or JPG depending on user preference). This is a potentially large number of masks to import later, so anything we can do to keep down the amount of work is a bonus to the speed of our export pipeline. If the host 3D engine can natively perform some function it's worth pursuing. In game development I firmly believe in the mantra "whatever works".

Summary

We looked at the detail layer stack and the two types of detail layers (Grass Billboards and 3D Objects). We went through each tool available to Detail layers; brushes, importing, and procedural mapping using distribution masks. Finally, we had a quick look at blending and the issue of baking shadows from trees onto terrain using object layers.

In the next chapter, we look at adding water features such as rivers, water planes, and a look at road building.

6
Water, Rivers, and Roads

Now we come to add landmarks to our terrain. From a player's perspective, rivers and roads are easy to follow, they guide us between places of interest. They provide barriers to different zones and give us something pretty to look at.

Water is one of those elements highly dependent on the quality of textures and shaders used. In older game engines, water was a simple 3D plane (or quad) with a reflective surface and maybe an animated normal map to simulate surface movement. Game engines such as Unity use this simple water plane technique. UDK features an actor that's capable of sophisticated physics-based water interaction; drop an object into UDK water and it sends dynamic ripples across the surface. UDK even does water refraction but these effects do come at a price. GROME is more like Unity, it uses a simple plane on which an animated material is applied. The basic water material has some nice options to adjust the color, opacity, and reflectivity of the water surface.

For our game we will rely on the game engine's native water effects (where possible), only the OgreGrome library (we will discuss in the final chapter) directly supports GROMEs water objects. But even as a placeholder we can use the water in GROME so we can model our scene.

At the end of this chapter we'll look at roads which are not part of the terrain modeling toolset but are part of what are called spline objects. A **spline** is a way of describing a complex curve using two or more points (what are known as *control points*). We can attach any texture to a spline object, plus they have the ability to deform heightmaps (with parameters for adjusting camber and width). Because of this we can use splines not only to model roads but also as a rudimentary terrain modeling tool for streams if we wanted. Let's put on our waders and jump right in.

Water layers

A water layer contains information about a water surface such as height level, texture, tiling, reflection, speed of waves, and so on.

Water is a simple plane object that fits the assigned zone, positioned at a height specified in the "level" parameter. By changing the "level" we can move the water plane up and down, intersecting the terrain.

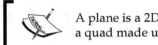 A plane is a 2D surface. The simplest is a quad made up of two triangles.

Sometimes in 3D engines that use water planes, ugly z-fighting artifacts are visible in areas where the ground geometry intersects the water plane, usually in the middle. This effect is more visible the higher the viewer is relative to the plane.

Terrain geometry close to the water plane is near coplanar (lying in the same plane), as a result of mathematical inaccuracies this can cause parts of the z-buffer to "fight" for dominance.

 The **z-buffer** is an offscreen area which stores the depth of each generated onscreen pixel. Almost every 3D system uses one.

Z-fighting is greatly reduced by using coverage masks, these work in the same way as any other texture mask. A water mask hides the water plane where it is hidden by terrain and thus avoids most of the z-fighting issues. This mask can be generated automatically using one of the procedural water tools which we'll look at shortly.

Creating a new water layer

Let's come back to the layer stack. As before we hit the drop-down control and set the layer stack mode to **Water** as shown in the following screenshot:

In this window:

- Click on the ⊞ (page) button to add a new layer.
- Ensure we have at least one terrain zone selected. Right-click on the layer and select **Assign to selection**.

This will launch the **New Water Layer** dialog as shown in the following screenshot:

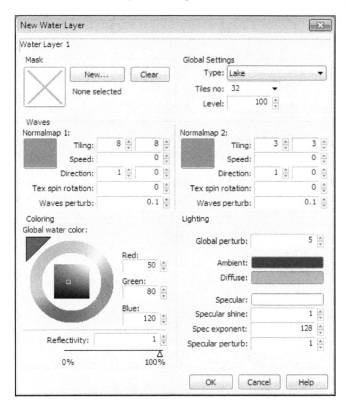

Options in this window break down into several categories: **Masks, Global Settings, Waves, Coloring,** and **Lighting**. All of these can be edited later but let's step through the settings here.

Masks

We use a mask if we don't want a solid water plane under our zones. If we click on the **New...** button for the mask we get the standard **New image** dialog (we've seen it before in other mask functions and it works in the same way). Remember, the color of the mask determines visibility, black is hidden, white is visible.

The resolution will determine how jagged the mask is. The default size of 512 is enough for most zones.

Global settings

The **Level** setting is the height of the water (or Y-value in the GROME coordinate system).You can change this at any time to adjust the height of the water plane. If you do, you may need to rebuild masks so they fit the terrain zone at the new height value. The **Tiles no.** value sets the tessellation of the water plane. We can keep this at a minimum.

Waves

The effect of water surface motion is created by scrolling two normalmaps (numbered 1 and 2) at different scales and speeds. By adjusting the **Waves perturb** and tiling values for both normalmaps we can get good variations of surface composition. The direction speed is a 2D vector (one value for each axis of motion).

The water in the following screenshot was created to offer a sensation of moderate wind over a large body of water. The settings are shown in the following table:

	Normalmap 1	Normalmap 2
Tiling	64	62
Speed	0.2	0.3
Direction	1,0	1,0
Rot	90	90
Perturb	0.5	0.5

These settings will produce an output as shown in the following screenshot:

Coloring

These settings adjust the color tint of the water. Reflectivity is an interpolation value between the water color and the environment map (reflective surface). When the reflection amount is set to 100 percent no color tint is visible. As we reduce the reflectivity, we begin to see through the water and the depths below.

One point to note, it's possible to have multiple water layers in a zone, we might want water features at different heights. If we do this, GROME has to rerender the reflection buffer for each one, so it's wise not to do that too often.

Lighting

Lighting options fine tune how the water shader renders global lighting with the wave normal maps. They permit the adjustment of bright specular coloring and ambient light intensity on water planes. Fine tune these for your scene, usually the default values can be left as is.

Shadows on water layers

If we have a material layer used as a shadowmap, we can apply the shadowmap to our water layers from the bottom of the layer stack. Expand the water layer and click on any of the children and you should see in the **Parameters** tab at the bottom, all the values we can change for the layer, including the **Shadowmap**. We can also use a material layer to add a diffuse color to the water plane.

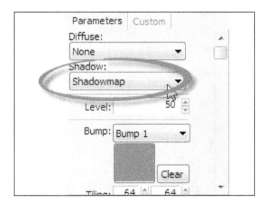

That covers the water layer, time to move on and run through the water toolset.

Water toolset

As with other tools, they are split into **Brush** and **Procedural** groups. Both feature methods to paint the water mask. The waterBrush tool is useful for touching up small areas as required. The Brush tool paints directly to the coverage mask on the water plane. But generally we will make good use of the "water generator" tool.

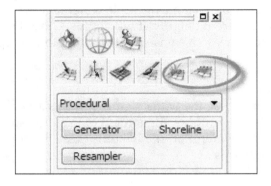

Generator tool

First button in the **Procedural** toolset is **Generator** which creates the water mask based on terrain height. Very simple to use, the only parameter we might want to adjust is **Depth attenuation**. This is how far in world units we want to see under the water plane. This is used to feather shoreline transparency.

The following is an image of a mask for a single zone, the dark areas are hidden. On the right-hand side is a 3D view of a zone where terrain has been flattened so that we can see the mask resolution along the shoreline.

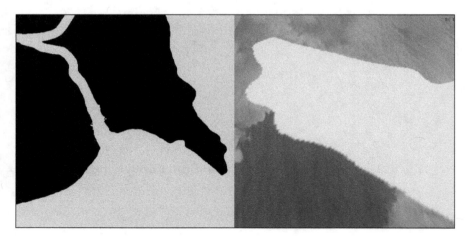

If the resolution of the mask is too low (or high), hit the **Resampler** button and set the resolution you want (remember to use a valid power of 2 texture size).

Shoreline tool

The final procedural tool is **Shoreline** which is a GROME/Graphite engine feature. This generates a lot of polygons around the detected shoreline and applies an animated "foam" texture. This doesn't export to other engines, some have their own system for achieving this effect and some are entirely done at the shader level and require no extra geometry. But it's nice to add that finishing touch to a water scene.

With our zone selected and the layer "armed", we can use the default values or even better, one of the presets, and click on **Apply**. After a short while we see the generated shoreline object as a red and green outline. The green lines are calculated normals of the shoreline.

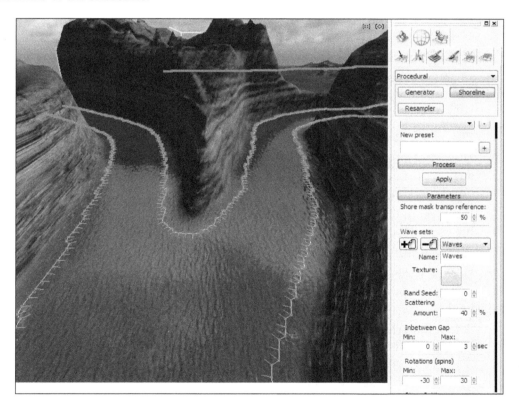

Creating rivers

Presently, there's no tool to create rivers or water bodies that flow downhill but there are a few methods we can use.

One approach is to use a plane, then switch to a heightmap brush. Using the brush we paint the path of the river, lowering the terrain below the water plane. This is simple and very much hands on.

An alternative is to use a selection, this is great if we have some real-world reference or diagram to use. Mark out the area of the river using a selection mask. Then use selection filters such as blur, extend, and smooth to give the area a more organic feel. Then, with the mask active, we apply the elevation tool to lower the terrain below the water line.

There are different ways you can work in river features and I strongly encourage experimentation.

Creating a small stepped river feature

One approach is to have a stepped river and use multiple water layers. These can be visually connected by using a waterfall effect in Unity or UDK. GROME doesn't yet have particle objects, until then we can use our imagination.

1. Pick a height value for our river. In this example we went for 256.
2. Using the heightmap brush elevation tool, set the level to 256. We lower the terrain gradually widening out as we paint the path of the river. Smoothing out the sides.
3. Heightmap brush Smooth tool; rounded of the "lip" of the waterfall where the river drops into a larger river below.
4. Added a second water layer at level 256.
5. Use the waterBrush tool (being careful to have only the new water layer armed) to paint the coverage mask. Fading out the edges closer to the river bank.
6. Add a material layer for the riverbed and banks along the sides, brushed to blend with the surrounding terrain.

In the following screenshot is a small river feature added using the steps outlined here:

For the Unity and UDK we will need to put in a lot more work to add convincing water features. Often games use particle systems to add foam and splashing effects and complex shapes for specific bodies of water.

Roads

These are sometimes and perhaps more accurately described as "spline" objects. Splines are curves defined by a set of control points.

Generally, these objects are difficult to export to other game engines. The COLLADA file exporter can save roads as 3D models, saving the triangulated mesh as model sections. The GROME plugin SDK exposes all necessary functions to get at them. Because we can't easily export spline objects as roads or models to other game engines, all we can do is quickly cover how to use them in GROME but we won't be using them later except as a guide for painting.

To find the Road tool we need to click on the **World** tab on the toolbar panel. Currently there's only one set of tools (**Roads**), the options are shown in the following screenshot:

World Editor projects are self-contained and can be used without a terrain surface. But when working with terrain surfaces GROME provides special layers for linking roads to the ground.

Create tool

Before we can create a road there's one important thing we must do; select the **New Shape** option in the tool box so a new road network object is started.

The tool panel rollup presents two methods of creating roads: **Points** or **Freeform**. **Points** is a simple, click a point on the ground to add a new road spline, control point, when you have two or more points GROME will connect them. Keep clicking to add more points.

The second method **Freeform** is handy if you change the View mode to "top down" (by pressing the *T* key) and then use the mouse to trace an approximate path around the terrain. GROME will smooth out our inputs and connect them as best as it can.

Let's create a road from the base of our river to the top of the peninsular.

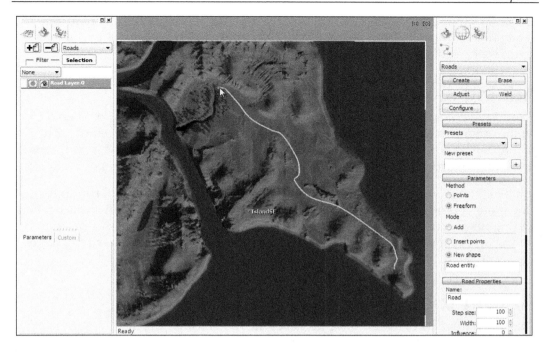

Once we've completed this we might find the generated road surface sticking through the terrain at various points. This is where we use the special and incredibly cool "glue" layer. I say cool because when I first discovered this feature I spent hours recreating tracks from the classic Amiga game – Stunt Car Racer. But, more of this later.

In the layer stack, if we now right-click our road layer and select **Assign to selection** we should see our newly created **Road Entity**. By default all roads are named the same. Get into the habit of giving them unique names so when it comes time to assigning the layer we have some idea which one we're selecting.

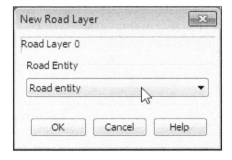

As soon as we click on **OK**, GROME will form-fit any terrain under the road, and this is where we can have some fun. Now the road entity has been "glued" to the road layer, we can adjust the control points to fine tune the path.

Adding more roads to create a network

To add roads coming off an existing road we set the **Create** mode to **Add**. Then click on the original road so that it's selected, continue drawing points in Freeform or by adding single points. Each new section of road will need to have its texture properties set so don't worry about new sections appearing in the default flat grey color.

If the new sections of road are not connected we can use the Weld tool to join them. One issue you might come across is that of gaps appearing in the road surface when adding new sections. This seems to be an artifact of how the engine is updated. Saving and re-loading the project will force a complete update which will fill in any apparent gaps.

Adjust tool

This tool allows us to freely move points of the road around the map. There are two methods of movement (see **Move method** at the bottom of this tool).

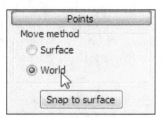

Surface and **World** are the two methods, described as follows:

- **Surface** will keep the point aligned to the surface of the terrain
- **World** gives us a 3D transformation gizmo which lets us pull the terrain up into the air or sink it into the ground

In the following screenshot, you can see a road point being dragged out to sea and GROME builds a "viaduct" to keep the terrain surface in contact.

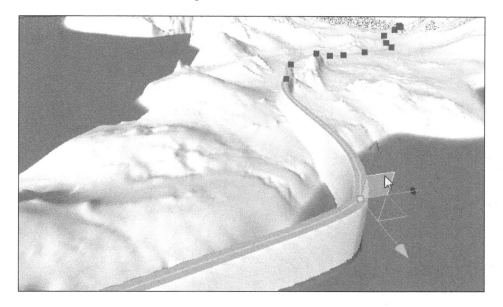

We can do more with this feature by applying a bevel to the road which will smooth out embankments and cuttings.

Configure tool

This tool allows us to choose road surface textures and adjust the width of the road entity. The level of control we have over a section of road depends on the active **Selection** mode shown in the following screenshot:

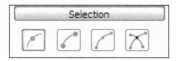

From left to right the modes are: **Points**, **Edges**, **Sections**, and **Network**.

For our simple example we'll use the Network **Selection** mode and click near the middle of the road (it should turn red). The road gizmo will be crossed at intervals by handles we can grab with the mouse.

Click and drag one out to the side, the embankment will stretch and smoothen out as you increase its distance from the center. If we click and drag the perpendicular line, we adjust the width of the road.

This is known as the "Influence", this is the amount of blending between the road layer and the terrain layer.

If we select the Point mode (the first **Selection** mode button) we can select individual points and make fine adjustments for the influence and add "bank" to the road surface by dragging the circular gizmo that appears in the image as shown in the next screenshot:

We can individually drag the influence control points which give this tool enormous flexibility for creating spline-based riverbeds. (Remember; the exported heightmap will retain the height information but not the road detail.)

One final parameter we haven't covered but should mention; **Step size** determines the resolution of the road. The larger the step size, the fewer polygons are used to construct the road geometry. When exporting the map in COLLADA format, the detail of the road geometry is based on this value.

Texturing the road

To apply a texture to the entire road network we should select the Network mode. The tool panel section called **Road Texturing** has three boxes for selecting textures (**Cross Out**, **Road**, and **Cross In**). With the road network highlighted, click on the middle **Road** image box ("**Channel source**: Road") which will force the package browser window to appear. A number of road textures are provided and filled in textures/roads.

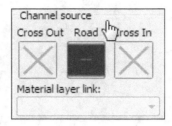

We can apply different textures to different parts of the road. With the "Edges" **Selection** mode active (that's the second **Selection** button) we can select individual strips of road (hold down *Ctrl* and click to multiselect):

 Using a texture with center line markings, for a "Dual Carriageway" effect, changes the scale of the "V" texture to 2.

Once we've built our road network, we might need to rebuild any shadowmap and normalmap materials.

Real road data

If we have real geographic road data in ESRI shape file format (and if you don't then you need to get it converted to this format) then we can use the "**Selection**: ShapeSelect" tool to import it as a selection mask.

From there we can apply the data to a material or heightmap layer (or both). Once we have the road system written out in rough and baked into the terrain we can work on it later in the pipeline.

Summary

In this chapter, we used the water toolset to create a simple water plane, mask, and shoreline. We also touched upon using several water planes to create multilevel water effects like the previous one. Then we explored the road tools, creating spline objects and using them as a terrain modifier.

In the final chapter, we export the terrain into three different 3D engines: Unity, Unreal Development Kit, and Ogre3D. Prepare for the final chapter, this is game development where some assembly is required and batteries are never included.

7
Exporting to Unity, UDK, and Ogre 3D

We're going to export our project to three engines. While Unity and UDK are game engines (although they certainly have uses beyond games), Ogre3D is a 3D rendering engine which doesn't have functions for audio or user input, but it's open source and quite flexible. We'll be taking a look at a the OgreGrome SDK which implements GROME's Graphite engine for Ogre3D.

Unity

By far the easiest of the three engines to use and can build games for PC, Mac, and mobile platforms. Unity comes with its own terrain system however this isn't available in the Unity iPhone/Android editor. This is simply because mobile platforms can't (yet) render the hundreds of thousands of polygons that typically constitute landscapes on their larger desktop counterparts.

In spite of this limitation, Unity iPhone/Android has been partly addressed by including a simple terrain system for mobiles, GROME still has this well in hand through its use of Mesh layers.

Mesh layers are 3D models based on the terrain heightmap exported in Collada (.dae) format. We can export our terrain with enough detail for a target mobile device or for PlayStation, XBOX, and PC. We can do this for multiple **levels of detail (LOD)**. For desktops we can simply use the heightmap from GROME and load it into the Unity editor so we can use all of the native Unity terrain tools for painting and vegetation. This presents us with two different export/import processes, one for desktops and one for mobile.

Desktop PC/Mac

The following method is the best means to get terrain into Unity for desktop applications, however we can't import vegetation or water features. With the help of a small script we can import four GROME material layers as Unity splat textures, directly. This also allows us to continue the edit process using Unity's native terrain tools. We can also create multiple terrain objects and import terrains into each one.

To use the native terrain tools in Unity we take advantage of the "RAW" data format. RAW is a 16 bit (PC endian), minimally processed file format that contains only data, there's no information about structure. When using RAW files we must know how many rows, columns, and channels of data were saved.

Export RAW terrain

The advantage of "going native" with Unity's terrain is that it comes with all the benefits of advanced LOD, texture painting, and vegetation details. Large terrains can get unwieldy to manage and a limited toolset means third-party tools are a must. For now, let's focus on getting a basic terrain into Unity.

First we export our data as RAW and make some notes on dimensions and cell size. We're going to export one GROME zone for each Unity terrain object to keep things simple. We can get information on the zone and cell size from the **Heightmap** layer stack (as shown in the following screenshot), click on the **Select** button and expand the tree view to see a thumbnail of the heightmap. The dimensions we need are shown as follows:

Subtracting 1 unit from the x and y value (because this number is the number of texels which is always plus 1) is 1,024 x 1,024. We multiply this value by the **Tile size** of **25.00** which equals 25,600.

This will be the dimensions (in world units) of the map we'll enter into the Unity editor for the terrain object.

Exporting from GROME

From the **File** menu in GROME select **Export**, change the **Save as type** to **General Large Data Export** and enter a filename (as shown in the following screenshot):

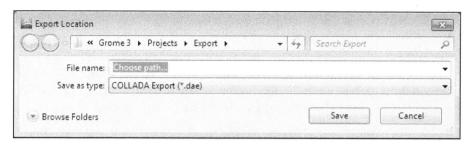

This triggers the appropriate plugin with a lot of options that are pretty self-explanatory. I will say that the heightmap should be set to RAW and the resolution should match the zone tile resolution. In our example, it is 25 units per pixel.

We will also check the **Vertically flipped** checkbox in **Terrain baked texture**. For **Terrain layer masks** if we check the **Export as multiple image channels** it will create a splatmap mask that we can import into Unity with a little magic, we'll get to it later in this chapter.

The **General Exporter for Large Data Sets** with suggested options for Unity is shown in the following screenshot:

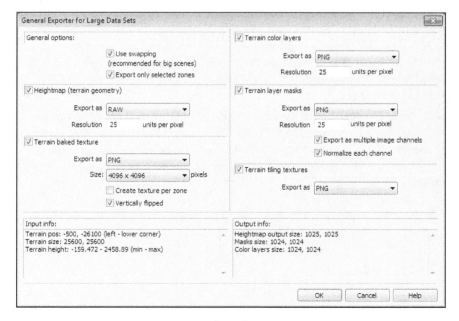

Importing into Unity

The following steps will allow you to import RAW files into Unity:

1. First create a Terrain object in Unity from the menu.

2. Set the position as required (the origin is usually fine unless we're planning to patch several terrains together).

3. From the **Terrain** menu, select the **Set Resolution** option. For our example, I've set the values to match our Island zone (as shown in the following screenshot). Our zone is 25,600 units square so to keep the scale we set the same values here. The next image shows this Unity dialog in action:

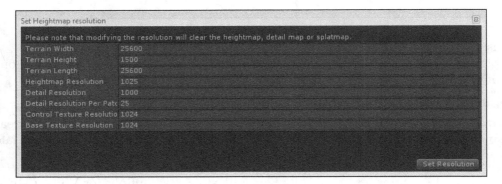

4. The **Terrain Height** value should match the one in GROME, you can get this value in GROME from the **Utilities** menu (Scene Statistics). When GROME saves a RAW file, height data is normalized against the height range in the scene. The full 16-bit range is used irrespective of whether your exporting gentle fields or towering mountain ranges. Also, Unity will not support heightmaps higher than 4096 resolution, if this is required, use multiple terrain zones.

5. Select the **Import Heightmap – RAW** option from the **Terrain** menu. Select the RAW file exported from GROME. A second dialog box will appear (as shown in the following screenshot), this is where we need to know how our RAW image files were saved, if we get these wrong things will look very strange indeed:

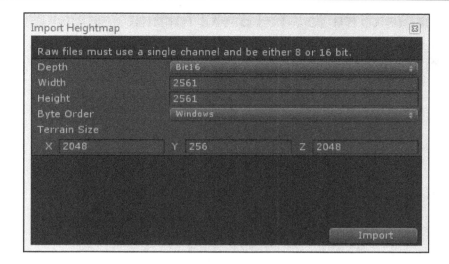

6. Make sure the **Depth** is 16 bit and **Byte Order** is set to **Windows**.

7. Click on the **Import** button and (fingers crossed, the Gods of graphic design are with you) the terrain will appear in the scene view. If it looks all spikey then you forgot to change the byte order (grin).

You might observe that the terrain is horizontally flipped, this is just the way Unity imports RAW data (if you load the RAW file into Photoshop you can see it's the correct orientation). While GROME will flip the baked texture for you, it won't flip the RAW file. If you have GIMP or Photoshop this is a quick edit.

Importing Unity Splatmaps

The GROME Raw exporter can create a `<export_name>_masks.png` file which has an option to normalize the output (this means pixels from all RGBA layers add up to a maximum of 1.0). This feature prevents over brightening of splat textures in Unity.

We can drag this mask file into our Unity project but we have to do two things before we can use it. First, we must convert it to **ARGB32** format in the Unity Inspector. Second, we have to add an undocumented function to the Unity **Terrain** menu to replace the terrain splatmaps with our new splatmap.

Convert texture to ARGBA32 format

Before we start, make sure we have selected the mask texture in the Unity Project explorer panel so that we can see it in the **Inspector** panel (shown in the following screenshot):

In the **Inspector** panel set **Texture Type** to **Advanced**, this will display all the options we need in the Inspector.

In the lower part of the **Inspector** panel, check **Override for Standalone** and set the size to the source size of the mask. Then set the format to **ARGB 32 bit**.

Click on the **Apply** button to finish the operation. Everything is now ready and we can apply the splatmaps.

Unity editor script to replace splatmaps

To add a new command to apply our splatmaps to the Unity editor saves this script as a JavaScript file (for example, `splat_tool.js`) in the currently active project's `Assets\Editor` folder.

```
@MenuItem ("Terrain/Apply Splatmap")
static function ApplySplatmap () {
  var splatmap : Texture2D = Selection.activeObject as Texture2D;
  if (splatmap == null) {
    EditorUtility.DisplayDialog("No texture selected", "Please select
a texture", "Cancel");
    return;
  }
  if (splatmap.format != TextureFormat.ARGB32) {
    EditorUtility.DisplayDialog("Wrong format", "Splatmap must be in
RGBA 32 bit format", "Cancel");
    return;
  }

  var w = splatmap.width;
  if (splatmap.height != w) {
    EditorUtility.DisplayDialog("Wrong size", "Splatmap width and
height must be the same", "Cancel");
    return;
  }
  if (Mathf.ClosestPowerOfTwo(w) != w) {
    EditorUtility.DisplayDialog("Wrong size", "Splatmap width and
height must be a power of two", "Cancel");
    return;
  }

  var terrain = Terrain.activeTerrain.terrainData;
  terrain.alphamapResolution = w;
  var splatmapData = terrain.GetAlphamaps(0, 0, w, w);
  var mapColors = splatmap.GetPixels();
  if (splatmapData.Length < mapColors.Length*4) {
    EditorUtility.DisplayDialog("Add textures", "The terrain must have
at least four textures", "Cancel");
    return;
  }

  for (z = 0; z < 4; z++) {
    for (y = 0; y < w; y++) {
      for (x = 0; x < w; x++) {
        splatmapData[x,y,z] = mapColors[((w-1)-x)*w + y][z];
      }
    }
  }
  terrain.SetAlphamaps(0, 0, splatmapData);
}
```

Once this is added to the right place (and assuming there are no script errors), a new menu option, **Apply Splatmap**, should appear in the **Terrain** menu .

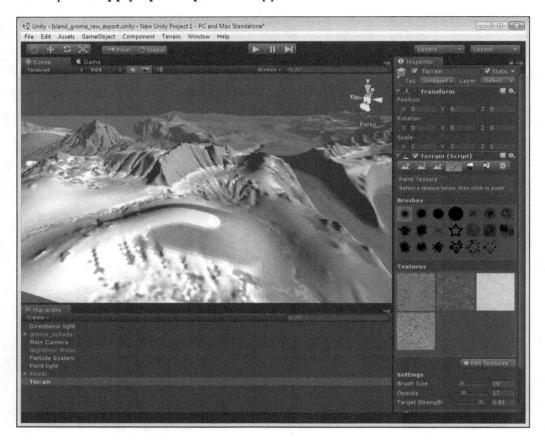

To use the function we first add four splat textures to our terrain object (as shown in the following screenshot), then we select an ARGB32 format texture in the project panel which will contain all of the splat information. Then we select our new **Apply Splatmap** menu option.

The terrain splat textures should then be distributed as per the information contained within our new splatmap. Our GROME island example is shown in the following screenshot after export in this manner:

We could improve this by applying our baked texture exported from GROME as the first splat texture, giving it the same x and y size as the terrain (25,600 in our example).

If the imported splats appear overly bright or contain odd color artifacts then the splatmap was probably not normalized.

Mesh terrain export

We can export GROME terrain as a 3D model (we might do this for devices that don't support terrain entities or a treadmill terrain system). Unity's native terrain tools don't work on such objects however navmeshes and colliders work fine. If we were making a flying game for tablets then this kind of export is ideal.

Getting the exported model into Unity is relatively easy since we can simply drag-and-drop exported DAE Collada files directly into the Unity project. From there we can assign any baked zone textures to it if required (the base texture is usually exported as a TGA and mapped automatically).

If you remember, we create terrain meshes in GROME using the heightmap's Simplify tool. This creates a representation of the terrain as an optimized irregular triangle mesh. However, if we don't manually create any meshes then GROME will export the heightmap as a regular triangle mesh.

Unity's **Inspector** panel has an **Optimize Mesh** which changes how triangles are ordered in the mesh. If you need collision detection on the terrain don't forget to check the **Generate Collider** option and click on the **Apply** button. (I've failed to do that once before and spent half an hour trying to debug a raycast *sigh*.)

The following screenshot shows an example of terrain exported as an irregular triangle mesh:

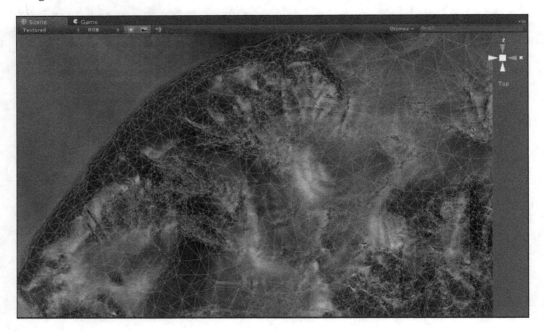

COLLADA is an industry standard format managed by the non-profit Khronos Group for the purpose of exchanging files between 3D applications. DAE is an acronym for digital asset exchange which is what we're going to do with GROME and Unity.

Mesh export from GROME

In GROME, go to the **File** menu and select the **Export** option to bring up the export location dialog. Here we set the **Save as type** to **COLLADA Export (*.dae)**. This setting determines which export plugin is fired when we click on the **Save** button.

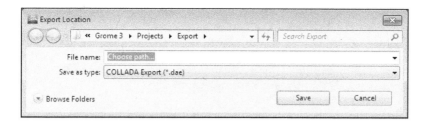

Set the filename for the exported DAE model file (something like `grome_terrain_island`). The export plugin will then display the dialog box shown as follows:

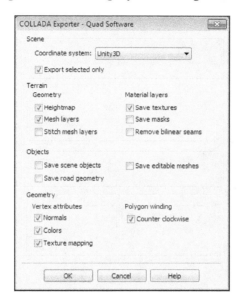

It's important we set the **Coordinate system** to **Unity 3D**. For our example, we'll be exporting multiple Mesh layers for use in our own LOD Unity script so the **Mesh layers** option should be checked, this will include each mesh layer as a child object.

GROME will only export textures and meshes if the "visible" icon of the item is active. We can use this behavior to control the output. If we want the normalmap saved into our export directory then we must flag it as visible on the layer stack. And the same for any of the mesh layers.

Road Meshes

Models exported using the Collada export plugin will contain meshes for any road (spline) objects if we check the **Save road geometry** box. This saves the road network in the scene as a set of triangle strips suitable for navmesh use.

It can take a few minutes to complete the save operation depending on size but once complete, we should have a DAE file and a series of .TGA format textures that we simply drag into our Unity Project window. Unity will crunch through the mesh and turn it into an object suitable for use in the engine.

The texture of the terrain will lack definition as the resolution won't be high enough for the terrain size (in the previous screenshot, the texture near the camera is quite blurry). The base texture will typically be good enough as a base if we're flying above it at high altitude but closer to the ground it doesn't look so great. We can improve things quickly by adding a detail texture. Select the terrain object Unity and change the shader to **Diffuse Detail** (this is shown in the following image).

We see the baked texture of the zone assigned to the base, now we add a detail texture; here I've used the same "mexico" texture from GROME and set the **Tiling** to **100**.

This adds some nice low level detail on top of the base texture and transforms the scene. Not all mobile platforms support multi-texturing so this isn't always available. The following is an image of the terrain model with just two texture layers applied:

If the terrain was exported with the mesh layers they will be present as child objects. Don't be alarmed if there's a lot of flickering caused by them being drawn on top of each other. These can be disabled in the inspector or deleted if we don't want them.

It's possible to have multiple mesh layers as LOD models, the GROME website has an excellent tutorial and example Unity script which swaps out terrain meshes based on camera distance.

If road meshes are present, create an empty game object and move them into it to create a prefab that's easier to manipulate. They are easy to identify as each road section is named "Road entity", the name of the zone and finally the instance number of the section. (for example, Road entity-IslandSE-inst 1").

When importing a DAE model into Unity it's possible (depending on the size and detail of the terrain) that it may have more than 65,536 vertices. This is the maximum most 3D engines will allow in a single object. Unity will split the model up into a prefab containing as many submeshes as are required for the entire model.

Unreal Development Kit

Featuring advanced rendering techniques, **Unreal Development Kit** (**UDK**) can now be downloaded for no fee for the purposes of trying it out. We're going to add a basic terrain object and import our GROME terrain with some texture layer information.

GROME export plugin for UDK

To export the GROME heightmap we will use a new plugin that makes it easier for us. It's important we match the plugin with the correct version of GROME. The most recent versions are given as follows:

- `http://www.quadsoftware.com/storage/udk/ExpUDK_Grome3.zip` (GROME 3.10)

- `http://www.quadsoftware.com/storage/udk/ExpUDK_Grome311.zip` (GROME 3.11)

Extract this plugin, ensure the .plug file is copied to the GROME3 plugin's directory (the source code is included but isn't needed unless you intend to make modifications). Launch GROME to install it. If the plugin initialization worked, UDK should now be an available option when we select export from the **File** menu.

This plugin creates a correctly formatted .bmp heightmap file which can be imported directly into **UnrealEd**. By default the height range is scaled to values between 0 and 65,536 which creates a lot of precision but we'll need to use the scale terrain in UDK. For the ground textures we will create four material layers in the UDK terrain properties dialog and pull in the exported .bmp files.

We'll need to check **Export tile textures** and **Export layer masks** so the plugin will dump all of the files we need into the destination folder. The tile textures are the textures used in the materials, the masks contain the distribution of that material across the terrain.

Once that's complete the first thing we need to do is bring up the **Unreal TerrainEdit** dialog box as shown in the following screenshot:

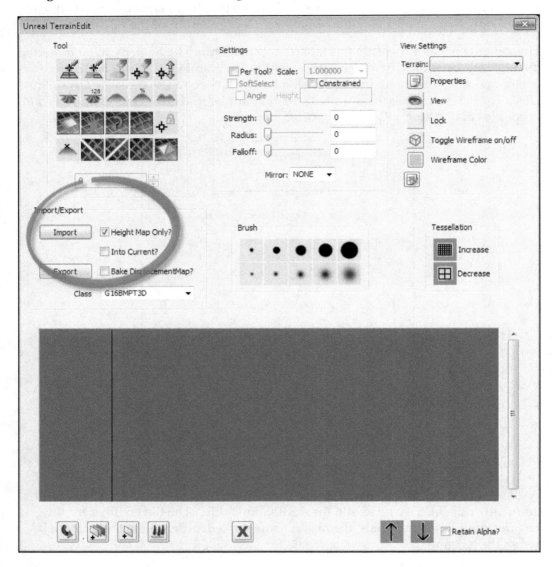

Here we click on the **Import** button with the **Height Map Only?** option checked and select the exported heightmap file. (This will be the name of the zone with an underscore HM suffix for example, IslandSE_HM.bmp).

This will take a few moments. If this completes the UDK layer panel should look like the following screenshot:

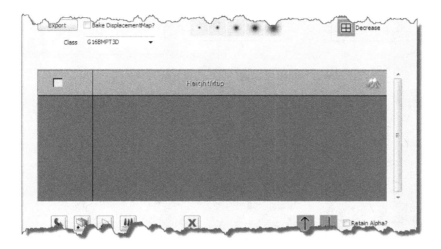

If the layer bar is gray it simply means this is unselected in the editor window. The scale of the terrain will need adjustment to make it visible in the editor, it will probably be a huge spikey mass at this point. Click on the "Terrain properties" icon and set the scale of the terrain to something suitable. In the following screenshot, I've used a simple ratio of 8 x 8 x 1 for our UDK map which is close enough to our original map scale:

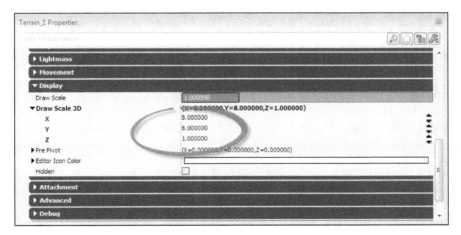

In the Unreal editor if we hit the *Home* key it should move our viewpoint to the terrain actor handle. We'll center up the terrain object in the editor and get to work on creating our terrain texture layers because chances are it looks like a blue lump of modeling clay as seen in the following screenshot:

To restore our original texture work is going to take a bit of time in the material editor. If you're not familiar with it then you soon will be. While it's initially confusing, if you've not had to work with shaders or material editors before then this is a cool place to start. It's such a powerful and creative way to experiment with new ideas.

If the terrain has too many points that are really sluggish, this is something that needs to be addressed by going back and splitting it up into more zones, or we can set the UDK Terrain Properties Tessellation Level to something like 4.0 (it must be a power of 2).

In the folder to which we exported our UDK files we should also have copies of our original textures for example `mexico03_tile.png`, `canyon_rock01.png`, and so on.

To bring these into UDK we need to add them to a package. From the Package Browser add a new package for materials. For this exercise, I simply called it `GROME_Package`.

Materials for the tiled textures used in splats will require adding a **TextureCoordinate** node. After we've dragged in the texture and added the UV **Textcoord** node the material flow graph looks like the following screenshot:

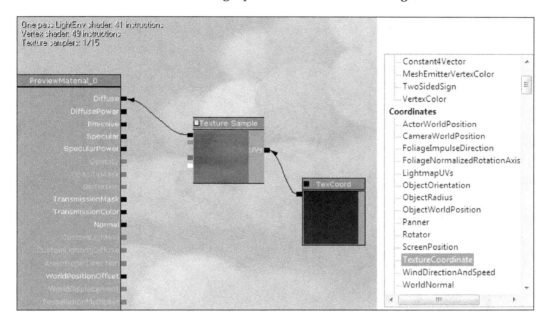

Our simple Island example has four basic splat texture layers, we will create four materials in the same way.

We can cheat a little by making use of a 4096 x 4096 baked texture and use this as a base like we did in the Unity example. This serves as an example of importing satellite terrain images and it delivers fast results. I set the UV coordinates for the base texture to fit the terrain (in my example I used a value of 0.003900 which overlaid the terrain perfectly).

The base texture alone isn't very good, at the very least we should add some detail layers and we can make use of the coverage maps in the next part of this example. The following screenshot shows just the base texture applied at this stage.

Additional layers can now be added and painted on top. The composite screenshot given next shows an area of our GROME terrain on the left-hand side, and on the right-hand side we have the same area in UDK:

UDK currently has no direct DAE import feature so we can't easily make use of meshes like we can with Unity. It's possible to use third-party conversion tools to bring in terrain meshes.

The only thing left remaining is lots of polish and fine tuning to make the terrain look like a million dollars. Quite often the fine tuning is a lot of hard work and there's no substitute (yet) for experimentation and a little bit of talent.

But I hope this text has gone some way to showing how we can integrate GROME 3.1 into our pipelines without any major difficulty.

Ogre3D

At this point I will assume you have some programming experience of the Ogre open source 3D graphics engine. A crash course in Ogre3D programming is a little beyond the scope of this book but there are plenty of great books and tutorials to be had.

Before we get started compiling a simple scene and viewer, we will need to install the OgreGrome SDK which at time of writing can be downloaded from:

```
http://www.quadsoftware.com/download.php?file=grome2ogre/
OgreGrome_1.00.27.exe
```

Alternatively, visit Quad Software's website and navigate to "GROME – Support for Engines and External Formats". There you will find links to any updated SDKs and plugins.

Another requirement is the OgreCOLLADA application (or some other tool) that converts COLLADA models used by GROME into the .mesh format required by Ogre3D.

http://sourceforge.net/projects/ogrecollada/

OgreGraphite engine

The OgreGrome sample viewer makes use of the Graphite engine and is fully compatible with scenes produced by GROME. As such, it is the simplest and most direct of the pipelines allowing the use of an unlimited number of terrain layers. Detail layers, materials, shadow maps, and object placement are directly supported as illustrated in the following screenshot:

The scenery shown is the demo scene bundled with the viewer. Ogre3D is a rendering engine, not a game engine, it works well with **Open Dynamics Engine (ODE)** for physics although the sample viewer application doesn't constrain the camera at all. Everything is left to the developer to add from other libraries. Ogre3D does what it does well (but some assembly is required).

Graphite is considered an outdoor "middleware" library and free for commercial and noncommercial applications — providing you possess a GROME license. Licensed users of GROME have access to the Graphite library which is needed to compile viewer application.

The OgreGrome viewer comes with full source and programming guide which will guide you through the process of integrating the Graphite engine with Ogre. If you already have a game library framework you will find Graphite easy to integrate as it's added to the Ogre rendering system like any other Listener class.

Exporting GROME scenes for OgreGraphite is the most straightforward export process, we will step through the process highlighting some of the main points.

Exporting with GraphiTE

The dedicated plugin we need for Ogre3D has a nice variety of configurable options. The good news is that these settings are saved, so we only have to set these once.

Starting with the **File | Export** menu option, select the **Graphite Exporter plug-in**, enter a name and file location and then click on **Save**. This will start the plugin UI, the first page is shown as follows:

We need the "Right Hand" coordinate system (Ogre uses a right-handed coordinate system). Click on the **Change Options** button at any stage to adjust any of the settings shown in the panel.

If you need images for a mini-map in your game, **Global** has a dedicated setting for exporting an overhead map for each zone. This includes lighting effects and ground detail objects. There are dozens of options available and too many to look at, most are self-explanatory. However, details of all the options are available in the plugin by clicking on its **Help** button. Most of the options are cosmetic in some way with the odd exception.

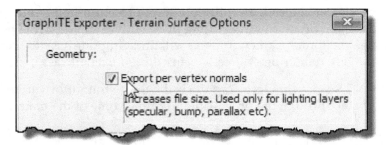

If we have a specular layer then we must ensure the **Export per vertex normals** checkbox is checked. The pixel shader requires normals from the terrain for lighting calculations, this also applies if you have any custom shaders that require vertex normals with your terrain. It makes the dataset larger and hence should be avoided unless you really need it.

Once we're happy with all our settings we can go ahead and click on the **OK** button to begin the export. This will take some time depending on your map size.

Once the export dump is complete, our destination directory should contain, for each zone:

- A `.tzone` file
- Image files for masks and any color layers
- Image files for detail objects (such as grass)
- Image files for roads and mini-map (if selected)
- An XML file containing model instances

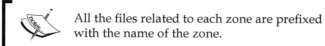 All the files related to each zone are prefixed with the name of the zone.

Use the OgreCOLLADA (or other tool) to convert any 3D models used into the native Ogre3D .mesh format. This will also generate the necessary material files.

Compiling the code

The sample viewer code can only be compiled if you have Graphite SDK library that is available to all licensed users of GROME 2.0. Preview versions of Graphite 3.0 can be applied for, through the Quad Software website at www.quadsoftware.com.

The source code for OgreGrome Viewer.exe is included in the src folder just below the bin folder. To compile, it's recommended you use the OgreGraphite.sln VisualStudio solution. Once loaded there will be some additional work needed for a successful compile.

You will need to set up the paths for:

- Ogre3D SDK
- Graphite source (available to licensed GROME users only)

The main source files in the viewer application are Viewer.cpp and Viewer.h. These contain all relevant code sections and cover:

- Initializing the Graphite engine
- Creating and loading individual TerrainZones
- The Graphite renderer Listener class
- Graphite shutdown

It's similar in structure to the standard Ogre3D example application so it's easy to follow if you're experienced at compiling Ogre3D applications. If not, there are several good textbooks on getting started with Ogre3D that cover compiling the basic example code.

Given next is the createScene() class member from the Viewer source code. This uses the loadTerrainZone() class member to load named zones.

In this example, `TerrainZone25.tzone` and `TerrainZone26.tzone` are files we assume have been correctly exported by the Graphite Exporter plugin:

```
void ViewerApp::createScene(void)
{
  // Init Graphite library.
  if(M_FAILED(initGraphiteLib(mSceneMgr, mCamera, mWindow)))
  {
    MessageBox(NULL, M_SZ("Error initiating the Graphite library!"),
M_SZ("Error"), 0);
    return;
  }
  // Load some terrain zones.
  _graphite->loadTerrainZone(M_SZ("../Media/Scenes/
IndustrialBuilding"), M_SZ("TerrainZone25.tzone"));
  _graphite->loadTerrainZone(M_SZ("../Media/Scenes/
IndustrialBuilding"), M_SZ("TerrainZone26.tzone"));
  // ...
// Load terrain zones associated object instance files.
  _graphite->loadObjectInstances(M_SZ("../Media/Scenes/
IndustrialBuilding"), M_SZ("TerrainZone26_instances.xml"), M_
SZ("TerrainZone26"));
  createGraphiteListener();
}
```

If a zone contains 3D models, a called is needed to `loadObjectInstances(...)` passing the exported instance XML document and name of the Terrain Zone.

Deleting zones

When we want to remove a zone including all model instances:

```
_graphite->deleteTerrainZone(zoneIndex);
_graphite->operateObjectInstances(gte::C_INST_OP_DELETE, NULL, M_
SZ("TerrainZone25"));
```

Going further – the edge of forever

The OgreGrome examples available from the website contain several tutorials in the following location: `Source/Samples/Terrain/DynamicLoad`.

I highly encourage readers interested in GROME to play with the "Dynamic Loading" sample, this is a solid example of efficient scenery paging in a large open world game. And building on that example is the "Dynamic Loading Origin Change" example. This demonstrates how to manipulate the matrix to always keep the camera and terrain tile close to the origin of the world. This is the basis of creating truly massive worlds not bound by floating point errors or similar or any of the constraints we discussed at the beginning of this book. Once these techniques are mastered there is no limit to the virtual worlds you can create.

Summary

In this final chapter we exported terrains as RAW and 3D models for Unity and used a simple script to import splat data from GROME. We installed a plugin for UDK and exported the terrain into the Unreal Editor along with material layers. Finally, we looked at Ogre3D and exported our scene for the viewer application.

Index

V

vegetation 80
Vertically flipped checkbox 113
vertical texture mapping 68, 69
viewports 18
Volcano Lair 11

W

water 93
waterBrush tool 98
water generator tool 98
water layer
  about 22, 94
  coloring 97
  creating 94, 95
  global settings 96
  lighting 97
  masks 95, 96
  shadows 97
  waves 96
water toolset
  about 98
  generator tool 98, 99
  shoreline tool 99
waves 96
white paper 47
workspace panel
  about 19
  layer stack 20, 21
  layer type selector 22
  scene tab 19, 20
  selection filter 22
  tools panel 23
  workspace tab 19
Workspace/Scene tab 31
world method 104
World Transform properties 36

Z

Z-buffer 94
Z-fighting 10, 94
zone
  about 24
  button 25
  deleting 136
  dimensions 26
  layers, assigning 56, 57
  procedural heightmap, creating 30, 31
  size parameter 25
  splitting 28-30
  tile size parameter 25
  tiles no parameter 25
  toolbox tab 24
zone splitter
  about 26
  example 26-28

Thank you for buying
**Grome Terrain Modeling with
Ogre3D, UDK, and Unity3D**

About Packt Publishing

Packt, pronounced 'packed', published its first book "*Mastering phpMyAdmin for Effective MySQL Management*" in April 2004 and subsequently continued to specialize in publishing highly focused books on specific technologies and solutions.

Our books and publications share the experiences of your fellow IT professionals in adapting and customizing today's systems, applications, and frameworks. Our solution based books give you the knowledge and power to customize the software and technologies you're using to get the job done. Packt books are more specific and less general than the IT books you have seen in the past. Our unique business model allows us to bring you more focused information, giving you more of what you need to know, and less of what you don't.

Packt is a modern, yet unique publishing company, which focuses on producing quality, cutting-edge books for communities of developers, administrators, and newbies alike. For more information, please visit our website: www.packtpub.com.

Writing for Packt

We welcome all inquiries from people who are interested in authoring. Book proposals should be sent to author@packtpub.com. If your book idea is still at an early stage and you would like to discuss it first before writing a formal book proposal, contact us; one of our commissioning editors will get in touch with you.

We're not just looking for published authors; if you have strong technical skills but no writing experience, our experienced editors can help you develop a writing career, or simply get some additional reward for your expertise.

Unity 3.x Scripting

ISBN: 978-1-849692-30-4   Paperback: 292 pages

Wirte eficient, reusable scripts to use custom
characters, game environments and control enemy
AI in your Unity game

1. Make your characters interact with buttons and
   program triggered action sequences

2. Create custom characters and code dynamic
   objects and players' interaction with them

3. Synchronize movement of character and
   environmental objects

Unity iOS Game Development Beginners Guide

ISBN: 978-1-849690-40-9   Paperback: 341 pages

Develop iOS games from concept to cash flow
using unity

1. Dive straight into game development with no
   previous Unity or iOS experience

2. Work through the entire lifecycle of developing
   games for iOS

3. Add multiplayer, input controls, debugging, in
   app and micro payments to your game

4. Implement the different business models that
   will enable you to make money on iOS games

Please check **www.PacktPub.com** for information on our titles

About Packt Publishing

Packt, pronounced 'packed', published its first book "*Mastering phpMyAdmin for Effective MySQL Management*" in April 2004 and subsequently continued to specialize in publishing highly focused books on specific technologies and solutions.

Our books and publications share the experiences of your fellow IT professionals in adapting and customizing today's systems, applications, and frameworks. Our solution based books give you the knowledge and power to customize the software and technologies you're using to get the job done. Packt books are more specific and less general than the IT books you have seen in the past. Our unique business model allows us to bring you more focused information, giving you more of what you need to know, and less of what you don't.

Packt is a modern, yet unique publishing company, which focuses on producing quality, cutting-edge books for communities of developers, administrators, and newbies alike. For more information, please visit our website: www.packtpub.com.

Writing for Packt

We welcome all inquiries from people who are interested in authoring. Book proposals should be sent to author@packtpub.com. If your book idea is still at an early stage and you would like to discuss it first before writing a formal book proposal, contact us; one of our commissioning editors will get in touch with you.

We're not just looking for published authors; if you have strong technical skills but no writing experience, our experienced editors can help you develop a writing career, or simply get some additional reward for your expertise.

Unity 3.x Scripting

ISBN: 978-1-849692-30-4   Paperback: 292 pages

Wirte eficient, reusable scripts to use custom
characters, game environments and control enemy
AI in your Unity game

1. Make your characters interact with buttons and
   program triggered action sequences

2. Create custom characters and code dynamic
   objects and players' interaction with them

3. Synchronize movement of character and
   environmental objects

Unity iOS Game Development Beginners Guide

ISBN: 978-1-849690-40-9   Paperback: 341 pages

Develop iOS games from concept to cash flow
using unity

1. Dive straight into game development with no
   previous Unity or iOS experience

2. Work through the entire lifecycle of developing
   games for iOS

3. Add multiplayer, input controls, debugging, in
   app and micro payments to your game

4. Implement the different business models that
   will enable you to make money on iOS games

Please check **www.PacktPub.com** for information on our titles

Marmalade SDK Mobile Game Development Essentials

ISBN: 978-1-849693-36-3   Paperback: 318 pages

Get to grips with the Marmalade SDK to develop games for a wide range of mobile devices including iOS, Android, and more

1. Easy to follow with lots of tips, examples and diagrams, including a full game project that grows with each chapter

2. Build video games for all popular mobile platforms, from a single codebase, using your existing C++ coding knowledge

3. Master 2D and 3D graphics techniques, including animation of 3D models, to make great looking games

UnrealScript Game Programming Cookbook

ISBN: 978-1-849695-56-5   Paperback: 270 pages

Learn how to apply an arsenal of essential and creative solutions for games using UnrealScript and UDK

1. Create a truly unique experience within UDK using a series of powerful recipes to augment your content

2. Discover how you can utilize the advanced functionality offered by the Unreal Engine with UnrealScript

3. Learn how to harness the built-in AI in UDK to its full potential

Please check **www.PacktPub.com** for information on our titles